"The Real Secret to Building Your Passive Recurring Online Income and Designing the Life You Deserve"

By Lance Tamashiro

www.IncomeMachine.com

Table of Contents

I Admit It... I Bought the Dream!

I admit it. I bought the dream.

I honestly thought that building a successful online business was easy, little work and would allow me not only financial freedom but also more free time than I would know what to do with.

I couldn't wait to buy a brand new laptop and sit on the beach while making money sending out emails.

My wife bought it too. She couldn't wait to spend more time at the Sundance Resort "doing nothing."

It was all so easy. While I admit I am not the smartest person in the world, I can usually figure things out after beating my head against the wall a few times. So I started building a list and my business.

Things were going great! Well except for the fact that I wasn't making as much money as I thought I would and I was constantly tired, overwhelmed, frustrated and confused. I was literally working 2 jobs and didn't feel any closer to financial freedom or personal freedom. The exact opposite was happening.

I rarely saw my wife or family. I didn't talk to my friends for weeks at a time. And for what? To be able to pay myself $2 per hour (if not less)?

This isn't the way the dream was supposed to happen.

It got even worse for me. My list had grown to a size that most people could not believe. It was even fairly responsive. I had learned how to make "just enough" from it. But it was nothing that could cover my bills, let alone take my wife on the getaway she had been planning.

I panicked. I could no longer justify the amount of time that I was spending on my "business." And that sucked because I could see that I was so close. I knew that I almost had it. I just knew it was within reach.

Then I looked at my "business." I looked at it hard.

I had a very big list. I knew how to earn some money from it, so I knew it was possible.

I was quickly becoming a stranger to my daughter Grace and my wife. I am so fortunate that I have a wife who believes in me and supports me. But this was NOT what was supposed to be happening. The dream I bought into was supposed to have me rolling around on the floor and playing with Grace. I bet she didn't see me 1 hour per day during this time.

I had no real product, something I personally made.

What? How could I not have a product? Isn't that just mandatory?

My business was empty. I didn't know the people on my list. I didn't give them anything special. What I did was just copy and paste pre-made emails and hoped people bought the product. My list could care less about me and the way I was treating them I was showing them that I could care less about them too.

I basically decided that I need something to change or I had to give up, which I didn't want to do.

I looked around me and contacted an expert in my industry. I told him I wanted to talk to him about my business and I him paid him to do so.

What started as a customer – client phone call has now turned into a great friendship and my business has changed.

He convinced me that I had all the foundation in place (the most important part) to create a new business, one that would achieve all of the goals that I had including more time with my family.

He convinced me that it wasn't hard to make my own product.

He convinced me that I could connect with my list and they would forgive me for my "copy and paste" tactics of the past and that I had lots to share with them.

I became laser-focused. Since that phone call my business has been thriving, I feel better about what my business is and most importantly I get to spend time all day long taking "breaks" and playing with my daughter.

Her current favorite thing is to watch Diego and make dad do what she calls the "Diego Dance." This basically means dad gets to jump around in circles and sing and laugh all ending with a big hug from her.

I also started getting emails from readers on my list. They were actually taking time out of their busy days to ask me a question or thank me for a recommendation or a product and a few times just to tell me thanks for the email.

It doesn't matter how many things I have going on in my business, I am consistently finding more time to spend with my family.

What changed? I watched what successful people were doing and copied them.

What did these successful people have in common? They are MASTERS of time management.

I started simple and took on 1, just 1 of my business partner's (Robert Plank) time management tips and got amazing results.

First, I started NOT trying to plan everything at once. Robert talks about his grandfather having "lists of lists he needed to make"… that was me. No wonder I had no time. How did I solved this?

Start thinking of your day not in projects but just tasks. I write down 4 tasks that I can complete in a single sitting each and then do them, one at a time. It is amazing how much you can get done when you aren't thinking about a million things.

In between each task I reward myself by leaving the office and going to play with Grace and spending time with my wife. Even if it is just 10 or 15 minutes. It's amazing how much quality time you have when you are able to focus on one thing.

Just Try It! It may sound simple and might sound stupid, but it works!

Try this one thing: make a simple of lists of 4 tasks. Not projects. And just complete those. Don't think about anything else.

You will be amazed at how much you accomplish in just 30 days and even more astonished after 6 months or a year.

This simple idea literally brought me one step closer to realizing "the dream."

Never Worry About Economic Insecurity Again!

I'm thinking back to just a few short years ago, when I was working in Corporate America.

I had spent almost ten years of my life, going to work, punching the clock, working from 8:00 in the morning until, if I was lucky, 5:00 or 6:00 at night, but usually more like 8:00, 9:00, 10:00 at night, for a boss that really didn't care for me, just moving pieces in a machine; feeling unwanted, feeling unappreciated, and feeling like what I was doing in the world really didn't matter.

What a difference in just a few years, what my life has become! What I'm really excited to share with you inside of this book is exactly how I went from being a slave to Corporate America to owning my own small business, working out of the comfort of my own home, and being able to enjoy and share more time and presence with my family.

All around me... friends, family, neighbors, people are constantly worried about how they're going to pay the next bill, how they're going to pay their mortgage, whether or not they're going to wake up and have a job the following day, and I understand this.

The big myth of Corporate America was that I never knew, from day to day, in both good economies and bad economies, whether or not I was going to have a job. It seemed like every single day, when I woke up to go to work, my job always depended on what side of the bed my boss woke up on, what budget cuts were being pushed down from the corporate headquarters, what price saving measures and money saving measures some manager decided they wanted to implement, so that they could ensure some sort of bottom line for the company and ultimately their own bonus at the end of the year.

Another thing that bothered me about working in Corporate America was that most of my time was unproductive. Most of the time that I spent working for my bosses and this big machine was actually spent trying to look busy, and maybe you've experienced this as well.

A typical workday for me, in Corporate America, went something like this. Usually, the main purpose of my day was to justify my job. What that meant was - as long as somebody saw I was at the office or somebody perceived that I was doing something and not causing trouble, then I would be rewarded with paychecks, bonuses, or sometimes even promotions but what was going on inside of me was something totally different.

I felt like I was completely wasting my time. I felt so often that I could get my real work done at my job in thirty minutes or one hour each day, and instead of completing the job and leaving I had to be there, punching the clock for eight, ten, twelve, sometimes even fourteen to sixteen hours per day all just to keep up this perception.

I became bitter. I got upset because a big change happened in my life, I had a daughter. Suddenly everything shifted. The money was nice, the money was important, we needed to have money to make our household run, but suddenly I found myself becoming very conscious about the time that I was actually having to put in and I felt was being wasted at this day job.

I started searching around the internet during work, and discovered there were people making a full-time income from the internet and from their computer at home.

Instead of finding meetings to attend to make the day pass quicker, instead of looking busy walking around the office talking to other coworkers, I found myself obsessed with the idea of residual passive income... meaning I wouldn't have to be active and something where I could actually supplement my income and eventually overtake my day job income while I was at work.

This was revolutionary to me because I had been trained that the amount of money that I was paid was directly proportional to the amount of time I spent working for somebody else; even if working only meant physically being somewhere.

What I found is that it is possible to not only build your own business and recurring, passive income stream while you have a day job, but also to work less and make more money so that you can spend more time doing the things that you love.

That's what I want to outline for you in this book. Exactly how you can go and build an online empire in your spare time, earning you $1,000, $2,000, even $10,000 a month passively and recurring giving you the ability to spend more free time with your family.

Internet vs. Offline Businesses

One of the things that first came to my mind when I was beginning to feel uncomfortable with working in Corporate America, when I was becoming uneasy with having my future and my paycheck in the hands of somebody else from day to day, is I started to look around at whether I should build an internet business or a traditional brick and mortar business?

Most people are familiar with brick and mortar or offline businesses and the problem that most people see when they think that they're going to build their own company or their own business and brand is that there are huge expenses involved.

You need to secure a building or a storefront, you need to secure merchandise or have it created, you need employees and most people, when they're starting an offline business, need to spend a ton of actual physical time at that business in order to grow it and make it run, especially when it's first starting.

This presents a huge problem for people trying to supplement their income or replace their current job with their own business. Most of us do not have the time to create a company and work for a company to keep our cashflow going.

Most of us do not have the bank accounts or the capital required to lease a building, to purchase employees and merchandise and the whole premise of having your own residual, recurring company or business is to increase the amount of free time that you have.

Working a day job and trying to build a business in the traditional sense really does not work for most people. Luckily, there is this new invention out called the internet and the great thing about the internet is that for a fraction of what it would cost to start a traditional brick and mortar business you can literally create a multi-million dollar company.

This has been done over and over and over again, where with just a small amount of time and investment, people are actually able to create full time incomes that support their families. Now, why is it so different on the internet versus a traditional brick and mortar company?

The first thing is that the start-up costs are much, much less. In fact, for about thirty dollars a month or less you can have everything that you need in order to run a successful online business. That's right, with just thirty dollars a month you can setup, create, and actually have all of the tools that you need in order to start earning an income online.

Think about how amazing and powerful that is because for just thirty dollars a month you couldn't do anything in the traditional business sense. Many people still have this idea in their mind that it's expensive to start a business when it's not.

The second thing that makes the internet such a powerful platform for starting your business is that you are able to reach masses of people that you could not normally reach with a traditional business. Here's what I mean by that. There are literally millions and millions if not billions of people on the internet today.

If you were to setup a shop in your local town to sell your widgets or your information or your guitar lessons or whatever it is that your passion is you would only have access to people in a surrounding area of your store.

Not only that, you would also need to advertise in order to tell everybody in the local area where your business is and get them to actually come in to buy your products or even find out about the products you sell.

With the internet all of that has changed. With the internet a small business owner, even a small business of one person, can now reach millions of people just by having their own website online and running.

Think about how that levels the playing field and how many people you could reach with your internet business. Again, I want to stress that you can get started with your own internet business for just a small investment.

The problem that most people have when they're getting started online is not the technical aspects or finding the correct products to sell, and we'll cover all of those things further on in the book, but the biggest problem that I see most people having when they're starting their own online internet business is their mindset. We're going to talk about that in the next chapter.

Change Your Mindset

The biggest problem I see entrepreneurs having when they're trying to start their own online business is not overcoming the technology issues. The technology is actually very simple and easy to use today.

It is not coming up with a good product. Having a great product because of the number of people online today and that you're able to actually find your perfect target audience is no longer a problem.

The biggest problem that I see people having when starting their own online business is a mindset issue. What I mean by this is that most of us do not know how to run an actual business. We don't understand how to be the boss rather than the worker. This is how we have all been educated and how we have all been brought up.

Think about your job. We talked at the very beginning of this book about my mindset at work and yours might be the same. We have all been conditioned to think that we are paid not based on how much we produce but how much time we put into something.

Now, I want you to be really honest with yourself and think about this just for a minute. Has there ever been a time at your job when your boss has asked you how long is it going to take for you to write a report or finish a project or create a widget?

If you're like me what you might have done is thought in your head, "That report will take me about thirty minutes." and then you looked at your boss and said, "That'll take me two weeks to get finished."

You might have thought about a project and said, "That project will take me two weeks to get finished." and you looked at your boss and told them it would take a month. The reason why this happens inside of working for somebody else is that there is no incentive for you to get things done faster.

There's no incentive for you to do a job faster. In fact, the opposite is true. You have actually been incentivized your entire life working for somebody else to take longer. The longer it takes the more you get paid. Most of us are paid by the hour.

Some of us are paid on salary, which means there's also no incentive for us to do things faster. We're paid the same amount regardless of how long something takes us, and therefore, we have all learned through working for other people our entire lives that it is better to do things slow and inefficient because we're rewarded with a paycheck.

Now that you're starting your own successful internet business you need to change the way that you look at your time versus your money. If it takes you five minutes to create something that pays you a hundred dollars, the amount of time you've spent versus the amount you earned has just gone up. You're now making more money per hour by doing things faster and more efficient.

Another thing that's very important when you're starting your own business is that you actually do things that move your business forward. Let me give you an example. When I worked in Corporate America one of the things that I always noticed and the joke among all of the workers was this: middle management doesn't know what it's doing.

Most managers, most bosses that we've all had, we look at them and they waste just as much time as we do as workers. But now what you need to do is change that mindset so that every single thing that you're doing is actually adding real value, not only today to your business but in the future for your business, because what we're looking to build is something that is residual and something that is passive, which means every single action we take needs to benefit us in the future.

One of the things that a lot of new entrepreneurs have problems with when they're getting started online is figuring out what to do when they no longer have a boss telling them what the next step should be.

In this book I'm going to lay out exactly how to start building your very first website, how to get buyers to your website, and how to build that recurring system but before I do that I want to suggest to you that you need to start thinking as a boss; as the CEO of your company.

Since you don't have money coming in yet you need to think that the quicker your employee – which will be you – gets things done (the more efficient you can be) the better your return will be in the future and the faster you'll be able to build your business.

I suggest you get rid of all your to-do lists and all of the things in your mind that you think you need to do in order to move your business forward and use a system that we call "Four Daily Tasks."

The "Four Daily Tasks" system is perfect for a small business owner just getting started because you have never thought in terms of being the boss, in terms of less time equals more money. Most of us naturally tend to find tasks that actually waste our time rather than tasks that move our business forward.

We tend to sit down and write a list of every single thing that needs to get done. We come up with pages and pages and pages of stuff that we'll never do.

If you've ever made lists like this you've probably experienced not having any of them get completed and you eventually get frustrated and throw out the list.

Most people like having lists because it helps give their brain the illusion that it is staying focused. You will experience something when you start building your first online business that people refer to as information overload or overwhelm.

Now that you're trying to be the boss and the employee and learn about how to build your own successful business you will have information coming at you at what feels like a million miles an hour from every direction and your brain cannot process all of that.

What I do in my business every single day is "Four Daily Tasks." Every morning when I wake up I sit down and I write down the four most important things on my mind that need to get done for my business that day. If nothing else gets finished that day I know that those four things will get done.

How do I determine what these four things are going to be? Three of them will be tasks that I can finish in a single sitting. For me, I can sit at my desk for about 45 to 60 minutes.

I pick three tasks, whatever is on my mind, whatever I'm thinking are the most important things that I need to get done today and write those three down. They have to be able to be completed in 45 to 60 minutes.

The fourth task is usually what I like to call a "gimme" task. That is a task that I can complete in ten to fifteen minutes. It might be something like sending out an email or running an errand or doing something that will benefit my business.

The key to doing these four daily tasks each day is each task needs to be measurable. If someone was to say to you, "Did you finish task one?" you could look at them and say yes it is finished, or no it's not.

I'm not talking about "finished" like what you tell your boss at your job, "Is that report finished?" and you say, "Yes, but I need to do some touchups on it. Yes, but I need to edit them." When you're running your own business you need to know if the task is complete or not so you can move yourself forward. It is either finished or it is not.

Again, you need to make sure that these are measurable tasks. For example, one day your task might be to secure a new web address for a website you're going to create. At the end of the day you can look at that and say, "Did I secure that website? Did I purchase it? Do I own the website? Yes."

One of your tasks might be to setup a new website at that address. How do you know if it's done? Well, somebody could go type it into the internet and find out if that address is there. It has to be something that is tangible and measurable in order to be finished.

The second important thing to remember about Four Daily Tasks is that there will be some days where you don't finish all tasks. When you don't finish a task this does not mean that tomorrow you do five tasks to make up for the one you didn't complete because what will end up happening is you'll be back to where we started - with this endless to do list that never finishes.

The key to all of this is keeping your mind and brain clear so that you can focus on the next most important thing that you need to accomplish for your business. When you don't complete a task, no big deal. Put it aside and start your day the next day, the same way.

You wake up and sit down and think, "What are the four most important things that need to get done for my business today?" If the thing that you didn't complete yesterday shows up as one of the most important things again today, then put it on your list.

What you'll find is, that by scheduling your day this way and by only worrying about the four most important things in your business that day, you will move faster and get more done for your business than you would by any other method.

Now that we've talked about why we need to have an internet business to build a passive recurring income and how we need to think differently now that we are going to be owning and running our own business let's get down into setting up our very first website.

This is the key to everything because if you don't have your own web presence online there is going to be no way for you to have visitors coming to your site, to be able to sell things to people or to be able to market either your products or somebody else's to your potential customers.

Setting Up Your First Website

I want to show you how to put up a simple website so that you can build traffic and see how simple it is to actually put something on the internet today that you own and that you control.

It really only takes a couple of small, simple tools in order to build up your online empire. What you're going to need is something called a web address, you're going to need web hosting, and you're going to need a website.

I'd like to use an analogy to explain how the internet works. Most of us are familiar with the post office or the postal system. I like to use this as an analogy so that you can understand how the internet works and why you need certain pieces in order to make your online business work.

When you send a piece of mail to somebody what do you do? First, you sit down and you write the letter and put it in an envelope and then you put on that envelope their name and address and then you put it in your mailbox. The postman comes and picks it up, looks at the address, and somehow magically knows from that address where to take that particular letter.

The same thing happens on the internet. When you go to the internet and type in an address, something like www.MembershipCube.com, into your web browser it automatically brings up the web address and it works just like the post office.

Your can think of your web address just like a physical, offline address. That is what your web address is. Some people will call it a ".com name" or a URL. Your web hosting is like the plot of land that your house sits on.

When you take your piece of mail and put an address on it, it refers to a physical place on the planet, a physical place that the post office knows to go to in order to find where you are at. That's what your web hosting is. It's like a computer or a physical place the "post office of the internet" knows about when somebody types in your web address.

The final piece, your website, is what exists at your web host or your "house". When somebody puts an address on a letter, it goes to the location, the physical location, and they can drop the mail off at your house. That's what's built on top of the land, or your web host.

We're going to set all of those up. The first thing that you want to do is secure your web address. To do that, you can go to NameCheap.com. When you get to NameCheap.com you can search for whatever domain (internet address) you want.

Your very first domain should be your name or the name of your company. For example, if I went to NameCheap.com I am able to search for LanceTamashiro, and it's also very important that you only buy the .com. Don't worry about .net, .org, .co, .mobi, any of those because when people think about an internet address they always think about the .com.

Put in your name or your business name that you're going to be creating and hit the Search button. Once you do NameCheap will come back and tell you whether or not the domain is available or taken.

Only purchase a .com name. If, for some reason the name that you're wanting is not available then you continue to search until you find something that will work for you.

When you're choosing your domain name it is important to make it simple so when you tell it to somebody it's easy for them to understand what it is. That's why your name is such a great thing to use for your first internet address.

Avoid things like numbers because people then do not know if the number is spelled out, if it's the actual number or it's something else.

A good example I see is people that will make domains like InternetBusiness4Dummies. What's wrong with that domain? The first thing is, I would suggest it's a little bit too long. Try to keep it short so that people can type it in and remember it easier, but Internet Business 4 Dummies – the 4 is actually very problematic; because is it the number "4"? Is it "four"? Is it "for"? You want to stay away from using those types of numbers inside of your domain name.

Another thing that you want to stay away from is repeating letters inside of your domain. For example, InternetMarketingSuccessSystem.com. I don't like this address, because SuccessSystem. There's too many S's all next to each other, so when somebody's typing it out into their web browser they're very likely to misspell it.

As a general rule, you want a short a domain as possible, you want to avoid numbers, you want to avoid repeating letters and you want to have things that are simple for people to spell.

Once you go to NameCheap.com and get your domain registered, you have the first step. You have your address on the internet.

Once you purchase your domain at NameCheap.com it is time to get your physical place on the internet. The place where your address (URL) can point to.

To do that I suggest you go to DoubleAgentHosting.com. When you get to DoubleAgentHosting.com there will be a button at the top that says "View Web Hosting Plans." You'll click on that and you'll want to choose the plan in the middle. It's called the Baby plan.

The reason you want to choose the Baby plan is it will allow you to host an unlimited number of websites. You can have as many websites as you want using this single plan.

Again, you want the Baby plan. Now, once you hit the Order button they're going to ask you if you want to register a new domain or address, or if you currently have a domain.

The reason why I wanted you to register your domain at NameCheap.com is you want to have your host separated from your web address. The reason is if you ever decide to change to a different host, if your business grows and you need a bigger, faster host, you don't want to have your address owned by the hosting company.

You want to own the address so that you can move it wherever you want. You will put, "I have an existing domain name," and enter your domain there. Then they will walk you through the steps of connecting your domain to that hosting account and you will then have your very own web address pointed to your hosting account.

If you type in your web address, nothing will show up because you have not yet built your website. You do not have a house on the piece of land that you've got but luckily there is a really cool piece of software that is free, called WordPress, that will allow you to create a website and manage your content very easily.

Let me show you how to do that. Once you have your website and your web host and your web address hooked up you can then go to your website's control panel. This is supplied with your DoubleAgentHosting.com account. You'll go to your web address cpanel (www.example.com/cpanel), this stands for Control Panel, where you can control what you put on your web host.

You can log in, and once you log in you'll get full access to a whole bunch of buttons. The one that you're looking for is called Fantastico Deluxe. It's down at the bottom. It's got a smiley face. It's called Fantastico Deluxe.

You'll click on it, and once you do, on the left hand side there will be a link that says "WordPress." You'll click on that link and then you'll click on New Installation. You'll have a couple of fields that you need to fill in.

The first thing is you want to make sure that it says "Install on Domain", and it has your web address in it. When it says "Install in Directory", you will leave that blank, and then you'll fill in your administrator username and password. This will be what you will use to log in and manage your website.

Then you can click "Install WordPress". Once you've done that, you'll get a screen that shows you where you're installing your WordPress. You just want to click Finish Installation and your website is now up and running. In fact, you can go to your web address (www.example.com) now and see that it is actually online and there is a base website there for you.

Log into your website and create new posts, you can create new content, and you can change the look and feel of your website by adding a theme to it and this is all managed inside of your WordPress site. Once you have your first site up and running you need to decide what you are going to sell online for your business.

What to Sell For Your Online Business

Now that you've got your very first website up and running and you know how to change the content, how to add posts, you need to make a decision about what you are going to sell online. Luckily, there are hundreds and thousands of products that you can sell very easily online, even if you don't have your own product yet.

If you're first getting started, the easiest way to start making sales and to start earning income is by selling other people's products. This is called being an affiliate for other people.

This is really simple to do, and a great way to start building your business. All you need to do is find a product that you like or that somebody else sells in an area that you have some knowledge about.

Important: the reason why you want to pick something in an area that you are an expert in is because then you can create content and talk about the products from an expert's point of view.

There are literally products in every sort of topic that you can imagine. We have students that sell products in how to draw cartoons, how to play the guitar, how to crochet, how to knit, how to build businesses, how to make model rockets. Anything that you can think of, anything that you might already have as a hobby, you can find products to sell.

If you're having a hard time deciding what type of product you want to sell, here's what I suggest. Think about what your hobbies are. Think about what you do already. Think about what magazines you might have laying around the house. You want to pick something that you already enjoy, something that you already talk about, because that will make it easier for you to write posts about those specific topics.

One of the traps that people fall into, after they've got their first website online, is they want to get into selling products that they know nothing about. Think about when you buy products, either offline in a brick and mortar company or online. You are looking to buy from somebody that you know is an expert in that area, so you want to do the same thing for your business.

If you spend a lot of time and know a lot about flying kites and know why certain kites are better for beginners or intermediates or experts, and you know what the best gadgets or accessories that people need for flying kites at different levels, then that would be a good topic for you to be in.

There's a couple of really great places to find products to sell, once you decide what area or what types of products you want to sell. One that I really suggest is called Clickbank.com. Clickbank has thousands of different products in different market spaces.

If you go to Clickbank.com, you can click on the tab at the top that says Promote Products, and once you are there, you can sign up for an affiliate account. You click on Sign Up Here.

Once you're signed up, you can then find all kinds of products that are available for you to market, simply by getting a unique – what's called an affiliate link, and sending traffic to somebody else's website.

They have products in arts and entertainment, in photography, in health, in dance, in fashion, in magic tricks, online gambling, business and investing, fiction books, games, green products. Everything you can think of, you can find at the Clickbank marketplace.

Once you've decided on your topic, you would go and find a product in that topic that you could promote. Then you put up content or write articles on your website, and embed your affiliate links and refer them back to those websites. If you make a sale, then Clickbank will pay you for those products.

Another great place to be an affiliate at is Amazon.com. Amazon has thousands and thousands of products in all sorts of different areas, from computers to health products, and they will fulfill all of the orders for you.

To find Amazon's affiliate program, you would go to Amazon.com, scroll all the way to the very bottom of the web page, and they have a link called Become an Affiliate. Now, once you're an affiliate at Amazon, any product that you find on Amazon.com, they will supply you with a special web address back to that product.

If anyone buys something, after clicking on that product, you will be credited for that sale and paid for that sale. There are a lot of product ideas that you can sell, even without owning your very own.

What a lot of people like to do is to create their own information product. If you are good on the computer already, if you are comfortable with setting up your first website, the next step is to create your own product.

Creating an information product is really as simple as writing a small how-to report. If you know how to crochet, then you could write a small report in Microsoft Word or in a text file, that explains how a newcomer would crochet their first hat, or crochet a scarf.

The reason why people like to create their own products, their own reports, their own books, is that you don't have to split the affiliate commission with somebody else.

Now, you do have to setup a more complex website, called a membership site, that we'll talk about in a later chapter. For now, just make a decision on whether you're going to sell affiliate products or whether you're going to write your own report or how-to information product.

Now that you have your product chosen, your website setup and you're thinking straight, we need to get you more traffic to your website. Now, the easiest way for you to start generating traffic to your website, and the first thing that you should do, is to start creating original content or posts for your site.

That's very simple to do with your WordPress website. In order to do that, all you need to do is log in to your website, and you will access what's called your WordPress Control Panel.

Log in with the username and password that you created, and you will be able to create new content by going to Posts > Add New. Create a title for your article or post and simply start typing, just as you would in any editor.

Once you're done, you hit the Publish button, and now your post or new content or article is now on the internet for anybody to find. Now, that's why I really encourage you to be an expert in whatever topic or area you're going to be selling products in.

The first thing you want to do is start creating articles with links to either your product or through your affiliate links to other products, depending on what you're selling. Another great way to get traffic to your website is by using Facebook advertising.

Facebook advertising is really great, because it's simple and fast to setup. All you do is go to Facebook.com and log into your site. On the left hand side of your Facebook screen, you will see a link that says "Ads Manager."

You're going to click on Ads Manager, and then you'll want to, at the top right corner, select Create an Ad. Now, once you do that, you will be able to choose the destination that you would like your ad to go to. That would be your website, the post that you just made, www., and then the post that you just created.

Then, you'll want to fill in a headline for your ad, and some basic text for your ad. Additionally, you can add an image if you have one, and then you get to choose your audience. Now, this is very important.

You don't want to just advertise to the whole world. You want to advertise to people that might actually like your product or be interested in buying your product. What I like to do is I like to start with the United States, and then you want to pick the age range.

I usually start at about 26 and let the age go as high as they want. I leave the gender at All – now, this is where it's very important. You want to choose something that would be interesting to the people that are going to view it.

Where it says "Precise Interest," you want to type in something that your ideal customer would like, something that they'd be interested in. Say we're going to be promoting a product on guitar lessons.

I'm going to type in "Guitar," and let's even see if "Lessons" shows up. There is, so guitar lessons, I can click and find out that I can advertise to 2,440 people, and it will only cost me between $.57 and $2.000 per click.

I know that every one of these people is interested in guitar lessons. Another thing I might want to check is let's see if they've got "Learn Guitar." Learn guitar, I want to learn to play guitar. Perfect, we'll pick that, and now we've got 13,000 people that we can advertise to.

Then, you can choose your new campaign, so we'll call this "Guitar." You can choose how much you want to spend. Now, I suggest that you start with $10 or $20, to see if your ad will convert, and if your product will convert. That way, you can test it very quickly and not have to spend a lot of money.

The suggested bid here for each click is $.60, so I'll make it a little bit higher and go with $.67, and then place my order. Once I place my order, Facebook will review and approve my ad normally within just 24 hours or less, a lot of times much quicker.

But just by setting up a fast ad like that, inside of Facebook, you can now access people and, most importantly, you can target your ideal customer by interests that they've said they like on Facebook.

Now that you've started to pick a product, setup your first website, drive some traffic to it, you might want to take it to the next level with something called a membership site. Now, membership sites are great, because they really act as your entire sales process, if you set it up correctly.

They will handle your customer support, they will deliver and protect your product online, they will take payments, and they will do this all automatically for you, whether or not you are around the computer.

Another great thing about setting up a membership site is that, in order to change the website that we setup, your very first website, into a membership site, you simply need to install a plugin called Wishlist Member.

Once you install that, you are then able to connect it to your PayPal account and create buttons so that people can now click a PayPal button that you own and purchase the product, and then be able to create their own username and login to gain access to your site.

The one thing I want you to think about membership sites is that they are great for taking not only what we think of as a membership site, recurring payments or monthly payments or payment plans, but they are also good for delivering just single payment products online.

The system that we use for our business to create membership sites and full training is available at MembershipCube.com. Now, basically, what you want to do when you're setting up your membership site is use this plugin called Wishlist Member. You activate it onto your WordPress blog, and then it will allow you to create membership levels, and they provide full information for integrating with PayPal.

What this will allow you to do is to take and collect payments and have the product delivered all for you, all on autopilot. The reason why I like Wishlist Member and membership sites is that I don't have to worry about collecting the money.

I don't have to worry about whether or not my product is secured or that only people that have paid have access to it. I don't have to worry about sending out emails to people, once they have purchased my product.

All I have to do is install one plugin into my WordPress site, called Wishlist Member, integrate it with PayPal, and now my product is protected and delivered, all on autopilot for me.

Membership sites are also extremely scalable, and what I mean by that is they're perfect for the beginner getting started online, because if you would like to start off by selling a single payment report, and your business grows and you would then like to start selling coaching programs or training programs or monthly payment programs, you can manage that all through the site, by just clicking a few buttons and changing the payment options.

I hope you are able to start thinking differently about your financial future, and understand that you don't have to be at the mercy of a boss or a company or a day job, that there are people making real money all over the world, using the power of website and internet businesses.

I want to make sure that you understand why you need a different mindset, that you are no longer getting paid for the amount of time that you put in, so finding the right systems and being as efficient as possible is now going to become your best friend.

I want you to go out today, setup your first website, make a decision about what it is you're going to sell, and start getting traffic so that you can replace your income and start earning that passive, residual income for the future that you deserve.

Step 1: Positioning

Degrees of Doneness

For years, I made a corporate career based on "degrees of doneness." If you've guys have worked in it, you probably did that too. Your boss comes up to you: "Are you done with this yet?" "I'm almost done. I need another week." That's how you made it through. For me, I would show up 30 minutes late, get my coffee, walk around and talk to everybody, sit down, go to a meeting and then my boss would check in on me. "I've been really busy this morning." Then you go to lunch and come back late.

That works really well in corporate America. It's almost setup for that. We're paid to be there, the boss is paid to manage people that aren't doing anything. If everybody did something, you wouldn't need the boss. The whole thing's setup for you not to be productive. The problem is that we are trained this way from the very beginning. We're trained this way in our education system, we're trained this way in the way that our monetary system works.

What happens is that people take and they translate it into "Now, I work for myself." I don't know how many of you are in this transition yet. I know a couple of you are but I know when I started working for myself I had to get my business license, I had to get my business cards, I had to get my phone setup and my office perfect because I was the CEO. That's what I saw the CEO of all of my companies doing, nothing, sitting around, making money.

The problem is when you work for yourself, every minute that you spend is a minute you're either paid for or not getting paid. The whole goal, for me and Robert, is I want to compress as much work time so that I can go and hang out with my daughters, I can do things with my wife, so that I can go play golf or do things with Robert or do whatever is going on but I need that work time to be work time.

When we look at what's happening, when we say "I'm getting paid X dollars an hour." We're looking at it like, if we do this webinar and we sell X number of seats, we're getting paid for that but what did it really take us? It took us 10 minutes to setup e-mails for 4 days, it took us 30 minutes to create a presentation, it took us 1 hour to do it, 30 minutes to produce the recording. Now, the intangible is we've got this thing that can sell on its own over and over again. That makes it sound really simple. You hear that and you're like: "Okay, I send some e-mails to my e-mail list. I do a webinar, I record it, I put it up and now it makes my pay forever." The reason why so many people can't take what I just said and make it a reality is that they don't have the base system in place.

The reason why Robert and I can do that is we've got these income machines built all over the place so every time we do something new, we just add it on, we just plug it on. What so many entrepreneurs do, when they come online is, every single time they've got a new idea, where they do a new thing, they start all the way over at the beginning again. It takes them a week to get their opt-in page, a month to get their sales copy, a week to get their membership site online. Robert and I look at it as we got this whole thing built, let's just plug things in.

Once you have this Income Machine built, what's really awesome about it is all these things that come into your e-mail start to make sense. When somebody says: "There's this great new traffic loophole that opens up." Robert and I don't believe in loopholes.

Every loophole we've ever seen, everybody we've ever met that's built a business on a trick or a tactic or a loophole is out of business within a year and you guys are probably on those lists, where you used to get e-mails from them and now they're gone.

What happened to them? They were telling you this great story and now they're gone. The problem is that they built their business on a loophole. Robert and I like to take advantage of loopholes but we also know that they're going to close down and be gone just as fast as they opened up. These websites like Google and Facebook, they're in the business of making money too. When a loophole opens up, you have to be in a position to take advantage, knowing that it's going to close down. You can only do that if you've got the whole system built up.

The other thing that we see a lot of people doing is they get caught up on things like "I want to be an author and have a book." That's great but what the most people don't realize is you make about $1 a book, if you can actually sell your book. Unless you're on the bestsellers for years, you don't make anything off of it. They're lead generation. If you look at most of the books that are on the market today, they're lead generation of some kind for whoever the author is.

The problem is that people will spend weeks working on their book only to find out they've got no back end setup for it. I'm not saying don't spend time on a book, I'm not saying it's not a good thing to have a book, I'm just saying: "Have the base in place before you work on that book." Because then, what makes it really fun, you can crank 4 books. If that's something you love to do, you got a place to send people on the back end.

I look my business as 3 pieces every single time. No matter what we're setting up, we're looking at how are we going to send traffic, we look at our lead capture part. How are we going to collect leads and what are we going to offer them? That's it. if you look at your business in these 3 pillars, that's every single piece that you will ever need to know.

Traffic, Leads, and Offers

When we look at that we have Membership Cube, which is our offer. The offer is membership training, the membership site, all that. We can look at it and say: "Is our problem that we don't have something to sell?" No, we do. We've got our offer. Then we say: "Do we have enough people coming to us?" We can look at that.

If you guys haven't, on all your hosts, you've got this things called AWStats in the back end, are you guys all familiar with that? You log in to your cPanel, on most hosts there's a whole section under there. It's called AWStats. On HostGator, it's automatically on, they keep it for years for you. Some hosts, you have to contact to turn it on but it's awesome because you can see what your true, unique traffic is and how many people are immediately coming to your site.

The problem is that most people come online and the first thing they think is: "I need traffic." That's the holy grail, that's all anybody thinks about but what they forget about is, they don't have any lead capture, they don't have a sales page, they don't have an opt-in page. What they end up doing is spend all this time figuring out how to run ads to send to an affiliate product. They spend all this time running ads to go who knows where. I'm not saying you shouldn't do those things, I'm not saying you shouldn't use those things but what I do this is, if I'm going to spend money on advertising, I want the lead.

Affiliate marketing's great, if that's your thing. We do a bunch of different types of affiliate stuff but here's the thing. Before we send them to an affiliate offer, we collect the leads. I want the list, I'm paying for it, I'm paying for that traffic and it's great to say: "I'm going to spend $1 and make $40", on the affiliate commission on the other end" but you're missing that whole piece in the middle, where you're not keeping that lead. If you're going to spend $1 on the lead, it's great to make $39 on it. What's even better is to be able to sell to that person over and over again. That's the lead capture part.

If you have all this setup it's great because that's what we're going to talk about is how all this looks. Also, you can figure out where the weaknesses are in your business. You can find out, I'm getting a lot of traffic but I'm not converting them into sale. Why? I need to work on my sale copy. I've got good sales copy, when people actually see it, it's converting great but I've got no traffic. The other thing is if you build this base system up the way that we're going to propose that you should, now all of this stuff, we think of our blog, we think of books, just the paid traffic source, your podcast.

We're talking traffic loopholes that people make public. You can now plug any of these in. If you've got anything in place, when it opens up you're easily able to take advantage of, whatever it is an plug it into the system without having to start from scratch. When I was growing up, my dad always told me: "You always want to be in a position to advantage of an opportunity." I never know what that meant. My dad was the kind of guy that would save up his money to buy a car in cash or save up his money and wouldn't do anything because he always wanted to have cash on hand.

You know they gave you these things credit cards as soon as you walk on to campus? I had all those. I was that kind of kid. I wanted leverage. The problem was that I then put myself in a position never to be able to take advantage of opportunities that came to me and I got stuck working to pay off bills where my dad, if somebody walks up to him with whatever offer he can go: "Okay, I want to take advantage." The exact same thing happened with your online business if you don't have to start all over again.

We'll come back to this but remember, everything in your business will fall in either traffic, lead capture or your offer. The best thing is that if you can get to the place where that doesn't change. Robert and I will go through once every 6 months and change up our offers on Membership Cube or change up our offers on Setup a Fan Page or redo some course but for the most part, once an offer's out there, it's there. We don't really go out and change much of our sales copy.

The process that we go through for writing copy and the way that we setup our courses and the way that we put things together, the copy writes itself. We're going to talk about that in a later session as well. People put all of this emphasis on "You got to have all this crazy sales copy. You got to use all these hypnotic patterns. You have to use all of these courses." You know what? Think about yourself. You're your buyer, if you would buy your product, probably your prospect would as well.

What do you really want to know? You want to know what's it going to do for me, what is it and how much does it cost? You don't care about all of this other crap, it's the thing that copywriters made to sell you copy. What happened was, you got to remember when a lot of this stuff started out, copywriting started because of print ads, because of things that they were mailing out, where they had to explain you this offer and get your attention or they would put them in newspaper or magazines. That doesn't exist anymore.

Today, somebody hits your webpage, they're going to take a look at it, they're going to make up their mind, "Am I looking for how to setup a membership site or am I not? If I'm not, why the hell am I here? If I am, cool. Does it solve my problem? What am I going to get? If it gives me what I want and I get more than what it's going to cost me, I'm going to buy it." That's just the way it works on the internet now. It gets lost where a lot of this copywriting stuff started because it was mass marketing. They didn't know who was reading their ad.

All they knew was, I put something in the golf magazine so they're golfers and now they had to try to appeal to golfers at all level, men and women. With online, we know who's getting there. Our website is targeted for a certain person to be there. When that certain person gets there, as long as it talks to them, that's all you need to worry about on your copy.

Too many people get caught in a loop. I remember when I first got started, it was like every time I got something done somebody would say: "Cool. Now you got to do this." I get that done and think: "Great. Tomorrow's the day I'm going to wake up and look at my PayPal and then I go, oh, I've got to do this." You feel like you're always chasing this thing. That's why we came up with this whole system because if you put this up, everything's there. It may not be perfect.

Robert and I really don't believe anything ever is perfect or ever will be perfect so just get it up there and get it done. One of the things Robert talked about is we don't have to do a lot of split testing because we know our niche. What so many people do when they come online is they want to get into something they don't know anything about. I remember that being really hard for me, when I got it online I wanted to be an internet marketer. I wanted to sell internet marketing training.

The problem was the only thing I knew how to do was to get traffic and build a list. I used to take training from Robert actually, when I first came on and said: "I want to do this. I want to be one of this big internet marketer guys. I want to sell all of this." He said: "But you don't know how to do any of that. Why would you go and teach that? Why would you try to learn any of that when you don't know any of it?" I was thought, "He's right!"

What he said to me: "But what you do know how to do is you know how to build a list and get traffic better than anybody I've ever seen. Why do you have to be this when you're already doing this? You already know the language of list building, you don't have to learn anything. You know how they talk, you know what their problems are, you know how to solve the problem for them. What got me caught up was I didn't see anybody else, at the time teaching that stuff. I didn't have a model, I didn't know how to go from, Robert's telling me that I should be the list building guy. I'm not on anybody's list that's a list building guy. They're all selling me all this other stuff.

Choose a Niche Where You're Already An Expert

The only thing I could model was these other people. I got caught in this never-ending loop. The most important thing when you're picking your niche is, do you have a competitor, do you already know it... The internet's a huge place, the world's a huge place. If you're good at chess and that's what your passion is, why the hell would you learn list building, other than to get more people to your chess site? You already know that, you already know there's a market in it. You already know where it's at and you know the language which gets you out of all the copy problems, you know where the people hang out, you know how they talk.

You really need to find a niche, whatever it is for you, whether it's NLP, storyboarding, being a doctor, whatever it is, stick to what you do best because it'll automatically shrink that universe of options for you down and you can use the credentials you've already got. That's the hardest thing. We work with so many student that come up to us and they want to be the next whoever, the next Frank Kern and we say to them: "Okay, what have you done? What's your big launch? What's your product? How do you communicate with your list?"

They say: "I have this idea." My response is: "You don't have any credentials, what do you do? What do you already have?" Because that's what people are looking for. You say you're good at chess, they want to know how long have you been playing, who have you taught, what have you done. It's really easy to get out of chicken and the egg right off the bat, if you can pick a niche that you're already an expert in. It makes the whole thing easier on you in general.

Think about what you can actually bring to table, not necessarily what you see other people and what you would want to be. There's way more money in doing what you already do. Chances are you already make money doing what you do, you already have systems doing what you do. Now, it's translating that. If you took time to learn it, other people do as well.

That was a huge breakthrough for Robert and I. The stuff that sells the most for us, the training that we get the best feedback on is the stuff that we bring, not the stuff that we're interested in and how we're going off and doing it, it's the basics. That's the part that people are missing. When we become experts in whatever our niche is, you need to remember there's way more people just getting started than are at this high end. If you build this thing up, you can have your offers to funnel them up to that but you always want to be focused on the masses, as much as you possibly can.

Once you have that niche, first of all, pick a niche and be there, whatever that is. Don't switch it around, don't go from chess to golf, don't try to manage all of this stuff. Have a niche, so that you can build out around it. Once you have your niche, then you're looking at getting your website and webhosting together. What we say by website is we're talking about your URL, whatever your domain name is.

Register your name. Whatever you're going by.com, whatever your name is.com. If it's available, grab it, if it's not do whatever you can. We even know a guy that had to change the name he went by to get the one but you want to make sure that you got that. The reason why is once your name gets out there, once your got products, people aren't going to be searching on your products, they're going to be searching on your name. You want to control those search engines about you, the search engine rankings about you.

One of the reasons we're going to talk about this why Robert and I put out so many blog posts for our products, we have blogs for SEO and it's good, we get some traffic from it but the real reason is nobody can stick stuff in the rankings about us that we don't want. We can control page 1 through 3 of the search engines off of any of our products. Nobody can put their review site in there, if people get upset and have to say something that we don't' want people to control or we have a bad experience.

We control all of that, we control all of the things on our name. Why? Because if somebody types in Lance Tamashiro, Google thinks they're looking for things that I've done or Robert Plank, things that he's done. Those are going to come to the top of the rankings first. Your name.com and then your articles are going to come up so you can control it.

The best search engine advice you're ever going to get, and the truest is, at the end of the day, if you don't want to worry about the Google slaps or Panda or whatever the heck they're talking about next, Google and Bing, they're in the business of, when somebody types in a search, the person gets the answer that they search for, that's it. They're not looking at keywords, they don't care what you have in there. They're looking at, did the person get delivered the content that they were looking for?

When I type up "How to get my hit my drive or straight?" The only thing that Google cares about, at the end of the day is did I get the answer I was looking for? How do they tell that? They know a lot of things. They know did I go back and do another search, did I go back and look at a different result? How long did I stay on that website? They know all of these things. If you want to avoid any slaps and all of these tricks where people freak out because they lost their business, play it long term. The search engine game's a long term game anyway. Give people what they want and eventually that's going to rise to the top.

What about heat maps? Basically, what that is there's some software you can install on your webpages, blog pages, whatever website and basically what it'll do is it tracks how far people go on your page, what they click on if they're on your page, where they sit on the page. What it does is it creates an overlay basically so they call it a heat map to see where people are at.

We used to play around with those years ago. The truth is the only metric I care about is did you buy or not. Here's the thing. Robert and I, when we first launched Membership Cube in 2009, we had a 50 page sales letter. We were like: "What we need to know is where people are dropping off, what they're interested in so we can give them more of that." We put this heat map on there, we tracked it and watched it. Every single time, everybody stopped, looked and clicked on this picture of a goat or a lamb that we have on that page. What did that tell us? Nothing.

All it told us was that it caught people's eye and they stopped there. That was it, it didn't increase our conversion. It doesn't give you any metrics that really matter. It's interesting, it's fun to look at but it's a marketing gimmick. It's something that some programmer thought "You know what would be cool, if people could see what was happening on their page" and then they make this big story about if you only knew where people were reading on your page but you don't, you don't know if they just stopped, you don't know if something happened and they left. You don't know what happened.

All you know is you've got cool blue and red overlaid on your website. At the end of the day, pretty much when we want to do any kind of split testing we use Google Analytics. They give you a code for the page that's a conversion page, a code for 2 of your variant pages and that's it. They tell you which one converts better. We haven't found anything that increased our conversion more than that.

Find the Bottlenecks & Read Web Pages Aloud

When we are going over our websites, this was a huge revelation to both of us. We actually get on a webinar together. Robert will give me the screen usually and I'll start reading out loud. Robert's watching the words and watching what I'm doing as I read. I would literally go top to bottom and start reading. A really interesting thing happens is I will start to use words and phrases that aren't even on the page.

We'll have something written out and I'll say it differently than how it's written. I don't know if you've guys have ever experienced this but a lot of time you read things and you know what it's going to say so you change the words just automatically, you don't even realize you're doing it. He'll have me go and he'll go: "Stop. You just said blah, blah.." and we'll change the text to match what I had just said out loud thinking that I was reading it.

That's a really good way to keep it more natural. I don't know if you read a lot of sales copy where you can tell this isn't how you talk, what is it? Nobody talks like this. Going through that process of having somebody read your copy to you, literally out loud, you'll change the way that it's phrased, you'll hear what doesn't make sense. You'll go: "Why in the heck would we say that? What were we thinking when we wrote that?" because you will type different than how you would read and talk.

I'll take the screen because he's a faster typist and better with technology. What'll happen is I'll read and he'll go "Wait." and then I hear him typing and he says, "Refresh." I refresh and all of the sudden there's images and all this crazy stuff. That's why we do it that way. For the most part because he's quicker with that stuff.

Have your name URL and then a URL for your product. That's it. The name of your product is the URL. The first thing that we do is come up with our idea, whatever the product 's going to be or the offer's going to be and then, we don't have a name for it. We just know it's going to be a backup creator. Somebody told us that kept bugging us make a WordPress plugin for backups.

We figured out how we were going to write it, how we are going to make the program, how it's going to work, what the offer was. The next thing we did, we said we're not going to go any further until we have the URL because what ends up happening, you branded all this way, you get to do all these PowerPoints, you make the product look a certain way, only to find out that your URL doesn't exist.

Then you're screwed. Then you come up with these goofy URLs like LanceTamashiro.com/BackupCreator/whatever that nobody can't get to or understand. Come up with your offer, then make sure you can get the URL of whatever it is. It need to make sense for what the product is, whatever you're going to be branding because that's how people talk. Robert just said who uses Paper Template. Some of you guys rose your hands. What do you think the URL is? The first thing you're going to think off is I'm either going to go to Google and type in "paper template" or I'm going to go to papertemplate.com. Nobody thinks I'm going to go to papertemplate.biz, papertemplate.net, paper-template... All of these things that people come up with.

You can buy those and add them on your domain but get the domain of the name of your product and it's got to be a .com. If that means you got to change the name, fine but make sure that it makes sense. We tried to come up with things that make sense for the product, sometimes we'll look and setup a fan page, we lucked out. My hoping, when I try to come up with it, I do it a little bit different than Robert. You can tell which ones I name and which ones he did. I think of what would somebody, if my mom was going to Google, looking for my product, what would see type in?

She was looking to setup a fan page, maybe she would type in "how to setup a fan page" For me, I name a lot of the products, as far as what I anticipate people would be typing into Google. I look at the Google searches and try to see what that is. Robert comes up more with actual names of products. Backup Creator, we just fell into.

If you're not going to make $3,000 or whatever on Membership Cube, what did we spend any time building it for? It doesn't make any sense, when you see people, they're not willing to spend $10 a month on a HostGator account, what business are you in?

We're in a unique position online, where our businesses don't cost anything compared to being on an offline business. We don't need an office space, we don't need furniture, we don't need all of this stuff. We got huge profit margins, we don't have to deal with inventory, most of us.

It's one of our pet peeves when people when people tell us: "I don't know. I'm thinking of this name and this name. I'm not going to spend $20 on a domain." Then they spend a week trying to figure out what domain name it's going to be. I'm thinking you could've just bought them both and park them on each other or you could've not shopped around for all the webhost and just got the biggest one on the planet that costs you $10 a month and have everything that you need.

If you're going through those things, that's what we're taught. We're taught do to that but your time is more valuable now. This stuff, these 2 things, get it done with so you don't ever have to go back and do it again. When we setup these 2 things for our income machines, we never go back to this, it is what it is. Now, the fun part is building up the traffic and making sales from it.

How to Be Successful

I've studied successful business people. I've read a lot about successful sports players and athletes. I enjoy trying to figure it out what it is and what makes the difference between some people who seem to always be able to succeed in no matter what it is they set out to do, and then some people who seem to fail no matter what it is they try to do.

Before we get into that, I want to tell you a funny story that led me into thinking about all this. Here is how it goes - the other night, well actually seven days ago now. Today is day number seven, you will understand what that means here in a little bit. My parents were in town, and my wife Martie who is this absolute health nut, she is a lot of fun, she's very personable and the one thing about her is she's got this weird way of constantly motivating me, pushing me out of my comfort zone. My parents are here, my wife's here and normally what we do after we have dinner is we watch some kind of movie, do something just as a family, just sort of hang out and talk. My wife puts on this show, I believe it was called Fat, Sick and Nearly Dead, something like that.

It's about a guy who is about 300 pounds, successful business person, but not successful in some area of his life, which was his health. Basically went he did was he went on a juice and vegetable fast, in liquid form - he did it for 60 days. Throughout this movie as we are watching it, he is challenging all these people, and I was really interested in how somebody could put their body through that. How they can stay away from pizza, and for me Wendy's and hamburgers, and beer and all that other good stuff that we all love.

We are watching this movie, and I happen to make the comment, and again this is on a Sunday - I think we had chicken wings, I had drank probably six to twelve beers, and I say well that looks easy I can do that for ten days. I didn't really think much of it, my family was thinking wow, you would do that for ten days. I come downstairs the next morning and she's got my breakfast ready. She had gone to the store, bought spinach, bananas, and apples. In fact, I am drinking fresh squeezed apple juice right now. If you have never had fresh squeezed juice, it looks a lot different than most apple juice that you see.

It is totally different, it tastes different. Basically she put me to the test. I asked, "Wwhat are you doing?" She said, "You said this would be easy, so you are going to do it." Silly me, right? That is the first thing, one thing that we all need no matter what we are trying to succeed with is somebody that can push us and motivate us to do the things we know we should do, and to actually follow through on them, accountability.

Here is what's happened, like I said today is day seven. I have had nothing to eat except for vegetables and fruit in liquid form, kind of crazy right. This has been one of the hardest things I have ever done in my life. Here is what I think is really important about this, what most people teach you about setting goals and about being successful, is to pick this huge "pie in the sky" goal. For me on this it would have been fast, drink nothing but juice and green smoothies and vegetables for ten days.

Believe me, almost every day I call my business partner Robert, I call my mom, I tell Martie, "I am quitting this, all I want is a Whopper, all I want is a Double with Cheese." This happens constantly throughout the day. What I noticed is that this craving, this choice of whether I am going to continue on the path that I am on to success or veer off onto another path, happens literally hundreds of times a day. Now here is my point with that, all I think about is what I am doing, what I am supposed to be doing, concentrating on it and when that craving comes up, when that choice comes up in my life daily, hourly, sometimes every couple of minutes as to am I going to continue onto the path to success, or am I going to quit.

I immediately choose which one I am going to take, it becomes very easy to know where you are going. Now if I would have started this process, all I was saying is I am going to go for ten days, it's not how I approached achieving the goal and I think there is a big difference here. Most people tell you, set a big goal, set a goal to have a million dollar company or ten thousand dollars a month, or run a marathon. They sort of leave you with that, and that is why so many people when they make things like New Year's Resolutions.

They are too big, they are a good "pie in the sky" but there is no practical way to actually get there. My point with all this, whether you are building a business, whether you are trying to lose weight, whether you are trying to get healthy - here is the way you approach it. Set your big goal, that's fine, but your big goal is not your focus. Your focus in on the small little steps that you are going to take in order to reach that goal, and if you just focus on what is the next step that you need to take. For me, it's every single meal, every time I get hungry what is the next thing I need to do?

I need to make a choice, do I go to eat fast food or do I continue on the fast. If I look at as it's the next choice, it's amazing how fast this "fast" has gone. I really encourage you to look at your business that way, I think so many people get caught up. They don't have a plan on how they are getting to where they want to go, and they are naive in thinking that you just set this goal and in a year you are going to be there.

Unfortunately, they don't do the steps that are necessary in order to get there. Just a little thing that I wanted to share with you guys today. I hope that this helps you, and I really hope that no matter what it is that you are trying to achieve, or succeed in, in your life you set that goal and then remember it's a constant bunch of tiny little steps. If you take those tiny little steps it will be absolutely impossible for you not to achieve your dream and goal. It will happen, take small steps, stay focused and just focus on the next task at hand and you can't help but succeed.

Step 2: Online Presence (Establish Your Web Hosting)

We use HostGator to host our small sites, it costs $10 a month. You can host as many URLs as you want on it. We do have a dedicated server, when you get ready for that we use a service called LiquidWeb.com. I think that costs us $500 - $600 a month. If you use HostGator or you get a dedicated server like LiquidWeb, quit putting these things on your WordPress blogs, like better security so people don't try to hack it and do all this stuff. First of all, you don't know who wrote that plugin and the number 1 way people hack your WordPress blog is by giving you a plugin with a back door in it.

That's the first thing, make sure you know who you're getting your plugin from. The second thing is a good web host has a thing called a firewall on their setups. What that means is they can tell when people are trying to access a website over and over again and they just block it. It's built into to every single host. Again, one of these marketing things that internet marketers made up so they could sell you a product is you need all this security stuff on your WordPress blog. What you need is to spend $10 on your host instead of $7 on your host and they take care of it for you. It's called a firewall, all your hosts will have that built in for you.

Once you have that stuff setup, let's see. We have our niche, you get to the fun stuff which is your opt-in page. Have at least or build yourself as many as you want. That's what's great about Paper Template is you can put something up there and build out as many opt-in pages just by copying the page that you've already got. The opt-in page, super simple. You don't got to overthink it. I used to take weeks to build my first opt-in page. Weeks, because I needed the right headline, I needed it to look right, I needed it to integrate right with Aweber.

The truth is, you just need a very simple headline, telling people what it is that they're going to get, you need 3 bullet points, that just describe what benefit they're going to have after they get whatever you trade them for and you need your opt-in box. Opt-in box is created for you by your autoresponder company, Aweber, GetResponse. I would probably recommend you stick with one of those two. They're the big guys in the market but you go in, setup a form, connect it to your account, they give you some code, either plug it right into Paper Template or you plug it right into your HTML page and it shows up. It doesn't have to be any more complicated than that.

You don't need all of this fancy stuff. We test this, we've had some of our friends test all this stuff. Every single time that we run tests on all these fancy pages, Paper Template, with just a simple headline, bullet points, opt-in form always out converts, no matter what the niche is, no matter what anybody's saying. You don't need the fancy graphics, you just need that simple page.

Why Your Business is Failing Online

There are 2 ways that I can approach this...

I can tell you what you want to hear. You know... you have probably heard some of these before:

- You're doing great building your online business
- All you need is to build a list and you'll be rich!
- Keep doing what your doing and you'll be living the "lifestyle"
- and on and on and on...

I know this is what you want to hear...

How Do I Know?

Over the last 4 days I built a new list of 2,426 new subscribers (we can talk about that some other time) so that I could do a little experiment.

I sent them 2 "personal" videos showing them concrete actions they could take to actually stand out to their prospects and customers with a call to action asking them to leave a comment about how they were going to build a better business and relationship with their clients.

I Got HUNDREDS of Responses

And I personally replied with custom videos and emails going into detail about personalized action plans each person could do for their business.

These weren't big things. Just small tweaks and tips that would get them better results.

Of the over 100 personal responses I sent I got less than 7 replies. I am guessing those were the few people that actually read them.

Anyone Else Confused?

Why ask for help and then turn your back on it? If you constantly feel like you are getting the "short end of the stick" online, maybe it is time to take a real look at your business and start finding ways to build it into the machine you want.

Now here is what you need to hear.

Building an online business is not as different as you have been led to believe than building one offline.

- You still have expenses, no matter what you have been led to believe.
- You still need an education
- You still need to do your homework
- You still need to DO SOMETHING that works

Here is the thing. I finally understand why SO many people fail online. They somehow believe that having a "business" online is like the gold rush.

They just push a button... money

They just build a big enough list... money

If the main focus of your business model is to "provide value" to your subscribers, I want you to think about the following...

HAVING to use deceptive headlines like:

- "PayPal Is Not Accepting Payments Today..."
- "re: You Purchase"
- "Your Commissions Have Been Approved"

Followed up by a "free offer" to get even more junk from another marketer is NOT providing value.

Don't get me wrong, these are fun to use and can be very effective, but this is NOT a business model, there is a big difference.

Second, hoping you can run a "numbers game" and get enough people on your list to click on a free crap offer and then run them through an endless cycles of upsells and exit popups is NOT providing value.

Are there places for upsells and exit popups and tactics like this? Of course! Just NOT the way you might be using them.

Take Responsibility for Your Business

It is about personal growth, relationships, passion and dedication.

- If someone led you down the wrong path... whose fault is that?
- If you bought into a scam... whose fault is that?
- If you're not getting the results you want... whose fault is that?

The good news is you can start changing these things immediately and your business and your happiness will benefit as a result.

The real keys to online success are actually really simple:

1) Provide REAL value, stand out and be yourself...
No one can duplicate YOU!

2) Study systems that have a proven track record from people that actually "walk the walk." If someone is telling you that you need to build a big list... do your homework and make sure they actually know how to do that. If someone tells you that you need a Facebook Fan Page with millions and zillions of fans. Make sure THEY have one. If someone tells you that you should build membership sites. Make sure THEY have successful membership sites (and not just the ones that teach you how to make one)...

3) Then rinse-and-repeat what ACTUALLY works.

Building an online business can be fun, profitable and extremely rewarding, but when was the last time you really got something GREAT without a little elbow grease.

Step 3: Lead Capture with a Forced Opt-In Page

We've some web pages, where we just had a headline and the opt-in form and that converts the best but least Lance and I still like to explain at least a little bit about what it is that they're getting.

The other thing to remember too, especially about the video stuff on opt-in pages these days is that a lot of people are reading your opt-in pages on mobile devices, so when you put a video on it, what happens on your mobile device? It's slow but if you're smart enough not to use Flash and something that all of them can see, as soon as you click on it, it opens up into a new window like on your iPhone. Then, where you're at?

We were looking at an opt-in form, sales page the other day and I'm on my mobile device, what should I do? I clicked a thing and it opened up into this separate window, I watched the video and when I closed it, it's like you already got the gratification of what you were looking for. Keep it simple. Again, stay in the mind of your prospect. Normally when people come to an opt-in page, they're looking for some information and they're looking for it fast, they're not looking to buy something.

You're getting them on a page where they look and they go: "Am I interested in how to make a recurring income? Yes. Oh, I'll learn how to use my computer to make recurring income. I'll learn how to setup all of my WordPress blogs so I can. All I got to do is enter my name and e-mail. Boom. I'm there" They're looking for that fast, instant gratification. They're not buyers on this page.

At the end of the day, they are hard selling their services, their speaking services. I would say test it but every single time, no matter what. We've had people tested in guitar, golf, list building. We've had a couple of therapists try it. The focus is on the copy or the offer, rather than on the bells and whistles. I would test it but I bet you that it converts better, that would be my thought.

All we keep is the form itself. All of that language that they put in there like: "We won't spam, we won't sell your stuff, we won't do anything." You're bound legally not to do that anyway, you can't do it. A couple of years ago, we had a pretty big marketer, we tested some of this stuff with and he was like: "Put it on there, it increases rate." All you're doing is, now when somebody comes and reads that, they're thinking: "Why are they telling me that they're not going to sell my information? Why are they telling they're not going to spam?"

As soon as you put it in their head, now they're thinking about it where they weren't at all. It's the same reason why we use short copy, jump links in our sales letter. What happens in a sales page, you read and you're like: "I'm buying this. I'm so into it." There's no jump links so you keep reading and then you're like: "I don't need to know that." You just talked yourself out of the sale. If somebody's ready to buy, under each section that's why we have the jump links so they can click on it, skips the rest of the copy, takes them down.

Facebook will do the same thing now. There's a difference between having a statement on the web page itself, because what Aweber will do, by default there's some verbiage that says: "We will not share or spam." What you do need to have for Google, Bing is getting there, Facebook just started requiring this as well, at the bottom you have to have privacy policy, terms of service, copyright, disclaimers.

Paper Template does this for you or you can find whatever verbiage but you just click some links down at the bottom. You can't hide them, they got to be able to see them. What a lot of people will do is, my page is white so I'll make the link text white so they can't see them. You got to make sure that they can see them. You just have those links down at the bottom of the page, they click on them and it goes to it. Everybody's going to require you to have that stuff.

Keep your opt-in pages simple. This is what gets people on your autoresponder. Everybody knows what an autoresponder is? Does anybody not know what an autoresponder is?

If you stop here, you're completely done. You can be completely done and still make money online. Why? I'm collecting leads into an e-mail database where I can contact them. You can completely stop here. You don't have to but you can. Once you get here, you never have to go back. Again, you can make as many opt-in pages as you want and continue it.

A Single Sale is All You Need

First off, I want to warn you. This is NOT for you if:

- are trying to "get rich quick"
- chasing the marketing dream of the "big hit"
- think "pushing a button" is a business model

Basically anyone who is not interested in building a long term, sustainable, REAL business... this post is not for you.

Ok, with that out of the way, I want to share something with you that can dramatically change your business.

Too many of us get caught up in the hype, watching the big launches and thinking that we are all going to become millionaires overnight. (I know I did)

The truth is these huge launches are not something that the majority of us can duplicate. If you have ever tried to get even a single JV partner (forget about all of the online marketing world), then you know exactly what I am talking about.

The way that it happens for the rest of us is usually a slower, longer process. The good news is that this gives us an advantage and allows you to build the foundation for something that is truly long-term and can pay you passive income for years to come.

I still remember doing the "happy dance" about once a week when I made a single sale.

A SINGLE SALE!!!

I recently polled my list and asked them... "On average, how many sales do you make in a month?"

Here are the results:

- **56.25%** of people make **0-4 sales** in a month
- **9.38%** of people make **5-10 sales** in a month
- **34.38%** of people make **11+ sales** in a month

Now there are two extremely important points about these numbers that I want you to check out...

Just Get Over The Hump

There is a group of people that are still "learning" how to make a sale online. That is about half of the group.

Then there is a very few that can between 5 and 10 sales.

And finally another large group that has figured out how to make sales consistently every month.

My experience was that once I learned "HOW" to make a sale online, it became easy to duplicate and I made a major jump in sales.

Just like the poll numbers show. Once you learn "HOW", the growth gets bigger and bigger.

Plan For Your Success

Most people never add a residual component to their product. This is a HUGE mistake!

Here is what I mean.

I am positive that each and every one of you reading this has a $47 product in them.

You should also be confident that you can sell a single copy of that product each month (even if you have no idea what you are doing)

That means that over the course of a year, you could expect to make about $564 on that one product assuming you ONLY make one sale per month (12 x $47 = $564).

That's 12 customers, 1 time

BUT...

What if you added a monthly, residual component to your product?

Now, each sale compounds and you can REALLY start building a long term business.

Suddenly over the course of 12 months those 12 customers are now worth $3666.00 (again assuming you only get one new customer per month).

Creating a recurring component to your product is simple to do.

What if you:

- Did a one hour call each month explaining more detail on your product?
- Used the questions from your customers to create additional videos?
- Updated the product each month with your new strategies?

I encourage you to take a step back from your business model and start to think about how you can maximize the sales that you are currently making and learn from the mistakes I have made with mine.

I can only imagine the size of my business if I had started with a recurring model to begin with.

Can you make a single sale of your product and build a truly passive income that will take care of you for years to come? I think you can.

Step 4: Schedule an Email Followup Message Sequence

Once you have that opt-in page up, the next you want to do is write follow-up messages. What that means is, inside of your autoresponder, you just setup first message "Thanks for getting my free report on why you need to back up your website. My name is Lance Tamashiro. Here's the link to that." Even if you don't have a product yet, you still setup this follow-up sequence. Why? Again, if you stop, you could still sell something.

What can you sell? I can sell affiliate products, I can sell other people's stuff, I can put them to a webinar. I don't need to have anything yet. Another thing that Robert and I do is, a lot of times we like to sell products before they're even created. At this point, if all you had was this, you've got this e-mail list, you've got this automatic messages going out to people so they know who you are. Big mistake that people make with their autoresponders is they're like: "I don't have anywhere to send them yet. I don't want to send them a message and tell them it's time." Here's the problem with that. First of all, what just happened?

Somebody came to your opt-in page, they don't know your name. They just know that they've got a free report on why they want to back up their WordPress site. They get that report, or not yet and then they go: "I don't want to e-mail them yet because I want to wait until the perfect time." When you reach your e-mail box, how do you decide what you're going to read? You look at the who it's from list.

People in e-mail copywriting get so focused on "What's my subject line? I need the perfect subject line." When I red e-mails, when my mom sends me e-mails, she doesn't put a subject line. When Robert sends me e-mails he doesn't put some fancy subject line. What I'm looking for is not the subject line, I do look at that but the first thing I always look at, think about your own. I guarantee when you open up your e-mail box, the first thing you do is you look down who sent you e-mails because you know right off the bat.

When people go "I don't want to send them too many" or "I don't want to send them any yet", you're wasting all of this because they have no clue who you are when you do send them an e-mail. Then you send them an e-mail and they go "A-ha, the spammer." It's like: "What do you mean the spammer?" If you send them stuff and say things like: "Thanks for asking for my report on this", send them e-mails. Even if you have nothing to say except for: "How'd you like the report? What was your favorite part about it? What did you think about it?" You're getting them used to seeing your name in your e-mail box associated with this. Now, you're becoming an authority on it.

Get people asking questions like: "What did you like best? How did you use it? What was your favorite part about it? What happens?" First of all, most people have to answer a question. If they're asked the question, it's human nature to answer a question but if they hit reply and answer it to you, you just got white listed in their e-mail logs. Now their e-mail system says it's not spam, you're sending messages back and forth. There's a 2-way communication going on.

That's why if you guys have been on mine and Robert's list for any amount of time, you'll see us. A lot of times before webinars we'll say: "Hit reply and tell me what you want you know about xyz. Hit reply and tell me what you thought about xyz." We do it because we want to know. We like to use that language back, we like to know what people are interested in but the real reason is that we're getting white listed in everybody's e-mail inboxes, we're not going to their spam anymore and if you reply to somebody, especially during a mini launch or something like that. We do a launch basically once a week.

If you respond to an e-mail where I say: "Hey. What do you want to know about setting up a membership site?" and you respond to it, are you going to read the next e-mail that comes back? Heck yeah you are, you want to see if the answer's in there. It keeps that relationship going with your e-mail campaigns. It's one thing to say, when we look around this room and go: "I know you and we send e-mails back and forth." but when you're talking about doing this with 10, 20, 30 thousand people they want to hear what's going on. It really makes a huge difference in your response.

If you get my e-mail in your inbox and you reply to me, it gets you white listed. There's a huge algorithm that places like Gmail, Hotmail and all of these systems, even the ones that are built in, some of you use the ones on your web servers that are built in. They're all social, they're looking at if I send 100 e-mails to xyz system and 10 people marked it as spam, they're thinking maybe this is spam but it's not spam for you, no matter what you do.

I'm on your white list now until you mark it as spam. The spam filters are working, it's a social thing. They're looking at what's coming through, what words are being used. I know you've been around this stuff long enough but people used to put f.ree because free was in the spam filters. "Oh, we're going to trick the spam filters by putting a space. Instead of saying money, we'll use some other symbol, money with a zero.

That's a trick but the real way to get white listed through but the real way to get white listed through so you can write whatever you want if you can get on somebody's white list. You'll see a lot of marketers that actually say things in their e-mails like "Make sure you add me to your white list." In the very first e-mail. I don't know where that is, in any of my e-mail boxes. I assume nobody else does either.

When you have a big list and people are responding to you, how do you respond back to all of them? First of all, when my list was much smaller I did respond to every single one of them. A lot of you were on my list when I would respond personally to every single e-mail that came in. Probably in 2009 and 2010 Robert and I would actually run campaigns where we would make video responses to everybody, so people would send us back responses and you'd get one of two things back.

You'd either get back a screen capture of us going through our e-mail, opening up your e-mail, reading your question back to you and then writing on the screen and answering it. I see people nodding their heads that have got this 3 years later in this room now. That built a good relationship. Some people in this room got video recordings. Janet used to get video recordings of Grace, of Marty running marathons, where they would have a 15 mile run.

I one way, I wish my list was still that small where we could take the time to do all of that. If you're in that position, make those connections now. There's tons of people in this room that have been, probably with Robert 5, 6, 7 years. Definitely people that have been with us for 3, 4 years now because of that because who does that? What we would do, real quick. You open up Camtasia, you record your screen, you just go through your e-mails.

I didn't know what they were going to say. Just open it up, read the question back to them, give them an honest answer, send it right back out to them. Now, what we do is sometimes we will write campaigns and we'll answers, as many people to come out and we'll say that in the e-mail, "I will personally respond if you do this." but now we use a lot of Burbage life, we'll answer this on the webinar. We'll make sure that it's answered in this particular place so that we can handle the objection.

Then, we produce the video in Camtasia, upload it in Paper Template, make a picture for them with Paper Template. We also have a script in video sales tactic. Basically, you can have 1 page and put the name after it and then you name the video the same. It shows so you can have 1 webpage.

If you're shy about sending e-mails, here's something to think about. If me and Robert go mail you, do you still get e-mails in your inbox from marketers? Your competitors are mailing regardless of whether you're mailing or not. If you're going to be the guy that's not going to bombard them, they're not going to recognize you and they're going to buy somebody else's product. Because you don't mail, it doesn't mean they're inbox is zero. They're getting tons of other messages.

The other thing too is that follow-up sequence. Again, this is in your Income Machine training, in the follow-up section is remind them that they download something, what it is. Your name's not here and if it is, they don't know who you are at this point. How many times have you gone to an opt-in page, download something, forgot you downloaded it, had no idea where you downloaded it, don't even know if you want to use it and all of the sudden you're getting e-mails from somebody and you're like "Who the hell are you?" You opted in to their list.

Send them a couple of days where you're saying: "I'm Lance. You asked me for a report on xyz. Did you get it?", "I'm Lance. You asked for a report on xyz. How'd you like the thing on page 3? What did you think about this? How did you use it?" because you're getting them used to knowing who you are and then when it's time, you know who you are.

Single vs. Double Opt-In

Let's talk about single versus double opt-in. There are two ways that the autoresponders are setup. The one is called single opt-in which means they put in their name and e-mail address and they're on your list and they get your download. The second is called double opt-in or double confirm. What it means they put their name and e-mail address and they get sent to a page that says: "You're not getting what I told you until you go back to your e-mail and click the link so that it's true."

I don't know anybody that uses double anymore. We've used single for years and years. The arguments that people have is people will put in fake e-mail addresses. Great, what do I care? They got my report with my links in it. If they like it, they're going to come back and re sign-up or go to my website anyway. Second thing what people say is you'll get more spam reports? I don't know if it's true of not , we have ...

No matter what you do, every time you send an e-mail, you're going to get a spam report. Somebody has a bad day and didn't want to see your message that day, you're going to go straight to spam. There's nothing you can do about that, it's part of the game.

Aweber will let you setup a list single confirmation. What happened was, when they first started letting people do that, people were loading up their lists through the single opt-in because you can't import. People were getting a bunch of spam complaints because it was spam, people were adding people's e-mails on their own list.

Aweber will switch you back to double opt-in if you get to many spam complaints but the truth of the matter is, if you're straight up , you don't any of this tricky stuff, where you're adding people and people are signing up, you're not going to be anywhere near that. I know we both run on sender score like 98,98% claim. Maybe I'll get 0.01% spam on any given e-mail. Usually it's 0.001, I'll get one or two per maybe 50,000 e-mails. If you're building your list right, you don't have to worry about it.

That's your follow-ups, get some in there, talk to them and get people knowing who you are. That's the biggest mistake people make with their list. After you got that setup, the next thing you want to have setup... You got your niche and website, URL all setup, an opt-in page with some follow-up sequences you want to get a blog up.

The first thing that I would do is I would either do a "ask campaign" or give them something big, if they don't know who you are. When I first got started, there was a lot of people talking about trying to learn list building at that time, what I did was I looked and I was like, all of these people are just affiliates, which is what I was. I didn't have products, I didn't do anything. I was like: "I want to do something where I can be a better affiliate, where people actually listen to me."

I would just do talking head videos and I would talk to people. There's a download page somewhere, Robert always finds that he likes to bring up. I'm in this dark lit room, audio's terrible, video's terrible, I got a baseball hat on backwards and it's basically just: "Hey. I'm Lance. Thanks for downloading this thing. It's right here.

If you need anything, let me know." I sold more product off of that page getting started than anything else that I did. It was because none of my competitors did that. Every one of my competitors just had a download page. It was link, link, link, buy, buy, buy.

I still had link, link, link, buy, buy, buy I just added a video where I was like: "I'm a real person too. Here I am." Anytime you can do something that appears personal or more personal than anybody else I think you're on your way.

Do you want to spend a month and a couple of thousand dollars making a 3 minute video or do you want to make a 3 minute video in 3 minutes? Your list, no matter what you think, the truth is your list is newbies. 99% of your list is newbies. They're just ... It's not attainable. When I got started, I saw those fancy videos. They were cool but I also knew I could never reproduce it. I didn't have the equipment, I didn't have the funds, I didn't have the time.

I'm the CEO now. I have 3 minutes to make a video because if I spend a month doing it, my company made no money and the payoff wasn't big enough for it to be there.

Launches

Stay away from long launches. You might see someone send a video, wait a week and then another video and then wait a week. What are you doing? If somebody sends me something, they're like: "Hey Lance. Here's this awesome video on how to make a membership site." I see the video and I'm thinking, "That is cool. I can't wait to setup my membership site." And I get nothing for another week, what am I doing as a prospect?

I'm out looking for how to make a membership site. You just made a sale for somebody else's product because you told them they had to wait another week before they're going to get part 2, and then another week before they're going to get part 3. I'm not saying you can't send out a sequence of videos but let them buy right way, if you're going to do that.

Robert and I, probably more than any other trick that we've got up our sleeves is, we let the marketplace for us educate the marketplace for us. When a bunch of people are talking about whatever this new webinar thing is, you can bet you're going to see us pitching Webinar Crusher really soon. Why? The whole marketplace is talking about this other alternative and we've got our feeling about is but now in everybody's mind.

We don't have to convince anybody that they need hangouts or webinars or whatever this new thing is. Our competitors have done that for us. We let them go and do all their stuff, it's on, "The whole marketplace is mine" and we swoop in behind them and clean it up.

One of our products is called "Backup Creator." What you don't see is, on a lot of our webinars people will say: "How does this compare to xyz?" We don't even entertain it. You see a lot of our competitors, for Backup Creator, try to complete with us. "We do this and Backup Creator does this. Here's our price and here's their price." You don't see any mention of any of our competitors.

Why? Because most people don't know any of our competitors. As soon as we put that out there, what's the first thing they're going to do? If I see a chart that's comparing 2 products, now I got to look at both products. I'm not just going to believe theirs and send in somebody else my best leads. It doesn't make any sense to even bring it up. Your competitors talk about you? Call them up and thank you, because even if they're talking bad about you, they're putting your name out there and they're making a comparison for you.

Step 5: Blog & Content for SEO & Authority

You have your niche, website, URL, opt-in page, follow-up sequence, you need a blog. We talked about, at the very beginning, get your own URL and have something up there. What we're talking about here is you want to have something where people can get more information about your product, then you give them articles just about that product.

What we do with these blogs, as we call them SEO blogs, social proof blogs. What we'll do is we'll have our URL, MembershipCube.com and we'll put it at /blog so it's a whole new WordPress installation just for this blog. What we'll do is we go out and get a whole bunch of articles. How do you get articles? You can get PLR stuff, you can have people write them for you. There are some really good article writers on Fiverr or you can do what this crazy guys does, he'll dictate out articles.

You talk for 3 minutes about something, you got a good 400 word articles. He dictates them out, you send them off to the transcriber, you can get 20-30 articles done in an hour. It costs us $20 to have them transcribed. Then what we do is we just load them into WordPress to come out into the future, every couple of days. What that does, same thing. First of all, if somebody's looking for membership site or they get sent to our blog and then that redirects them back to the sales page but now, we also we're controlling, he puts out 100 articles on our blog, people start searching for our stuff, we got a ton of results.

The first thing people think is "Wow, these guys must be the only guys that teach membership sites because that's all I'm seeing in the search results." It also it keeps out people that are keywords stuff in against us because we're controlling it. It's on when they're search for "Membership Cube" or "Lance and Robert Membership Cube" We control the first couple of pages just by having these articles dripped out.

Again, what we do is we'll come up with just a bunch of ideas for topics that we want to have, dictate them out. We don't think about how many times we say the word membership site. The way that we make our articles is, it's a question. It's like "How do I setup a membership site?" That'll literally be the topic and you just answer the question. What does that do? When somebody goes to Google, you know you're giving Google what they want and you're talking like a regular person, so you get the rankings.

Go to your AWstats and you can find out what words are you ranking for. It's called reverse SEO. Put a bunch of stuff out there, when you start to rank for certain types of words at Google or Bing, things that you're giving good content about, that's when you write more articles on that particular subject, rather than trying to trick them by saying the word 4 times or by adding in a phrase a certain number of times. What they're looking for is, when somebody types in a response and they send them there, are they getting the answer they're looking for?

The Secret to Selling More Products

I want to spend some time talking about how you can sell more products online. Whether you are trying to write sales pages and sales copy, or whether you are just trying to sell products through Webinars, and how to actually get everything to flow, so that people are more compelled to purchase your products.

Look, it's no secret. When you come online one of the things that most of us get help up with, I know it was true for me, I didn't realize there was this whole thing called "copywriting."

I didn't realize that I was going to have to learn, not only how to lay things out and make them look pretty on a web page, but the words that I say were important as well.

And what happened to me was this was a big hold up. In fact, it stopped me from creating sales pages and from selling high dollar products for a very long time. I thought I had to master this thing called "copywriting."

And so I went through looking for people to teach me copywriting. I found a bunch of $500, $1,000, $2,400 courses that I could go through where people would teach me this skill.

And here's what I found. By buying all these courses, it wasn't actually putting me closer to my goal, which was getting my sales letter online, and my sales message together so that I could sell something.

It was actually causing a lot more confusion in my head about what I was I was supposed to be doing. And it put a lot of doubt inside of me that I could sell anything at all. In fact, I thought I wasn't going to be able to sell anything, because I couldn't master this thing called 'copywriting.'

So I ended up spending a whole bunch of money. I ended up wasting a whole bunch of time. And I ended up setting myself back, instead of moving myself forward. Because I started putting all these fears and doubts about whether or not I could sell something in my head.

I knew I had a great product. I knew I had things that I could teach people. I just didn't know how to put that sales message together. So I found a whole lot of "advice." I going to use this term loosely. 'Advice' about what I should do to become better at writing sales, and better at making sales presentations for Webinars. And I ran this thing called 'copyright.'

Here's some of the advice I got. And maybe you've heard some of this, and maybe some of this advice is what held you up as well.

One of the big things that I came upon was that I needed to buy somebody's copywriting course. I'm not saying that the copywriting course is not good, and there are not things to learn. I'm just saying that when I was first getting started they weren't of any help to me.

Now once you get going, once you have something that sells, once you understand the basics of what it is that you need to have on your sales page and you can write a simple short letter that converts, then I think that these copywriting course are great. Because then you will pick up little tips and tricks. You will pick up little things that you can say that worked better.

But I think for the person just getting started, they are just flat out overwhelming.

So here is what I would say, Instead of going out a buying a huge copywriting course right off the bat, I would suggest that you just start paying attention to what it is that makes you buy.

Think about it! If you are listening to this podcast, chances are that you bought something online.

Whether it is something off of Amazon, eBay, a traditional sales letter, a Webinar, a video sales letter, it really doesn't matter, you have probably purchased something online.

What I want you to start paying attention to, not by taking notes, having a Journal, or by note-book, or a Swipe File. You just need to pay attention to the things that keep coming up over and over again that are helping to push you to buy.

If you start paying attention to what it is that actually makes you decide to make a purchase versus not to make a purchase, I bet you it always comes down to the same thing. Think about it! What is it that makes you buy? What is it that actually makes you click the "Buy" button for something online, or on a Webinar?

It's the result that you are going to get making that purchase, versus the price of what the purchase is.

Here is what I mean: If you are on eBay and you are looking to get a concert ticket that you can't get into. The price of the ticket is $100 and you feel that you really need to go to that concert, it makes the buying easy right? What do you get? You get to go to a concert, now you just have to evaluate the price for it.

Or, if you are buying a WordPress plug-in off of a sales letter online. What is it that makes you buy? I guarantee you that at end the end of the day what makes you buy is: What benefit do you get from that WordPress plug-in versus the price.

For a lot of us that's a time issue, I could buy a WordPress plug-in, like Paper Template, that easily lets me setup a sales page, gives me a cut and paste template that already exists and I just fill in the blanks for $47. I look at that and say "Just to do the layout myself it would take me 2-3 hours to get it all right, is that worth $47 for just that one piece, yes."

If you're looking to buy a course for something, or to learn something, what is it that makes you determine whether or not you are going to buy? Well it's probably, where am I at today, what will that course teach me, what will I have learned by the end of it, and, is it worth a certain amount of money?

Think in terms of that when you're thinking about your sales message, your prospects are no different from you when they purchase something. They want to know whether or not the benefit of what they are going to receive after purchasing your product, your service, your goods, whatever it is, will the result of it be worth more than the cost. And if it is, you have an easy sale to make.

So don't think right off the bat about these huge copywriting courses. What it really boils down to is, can you show people the benefit they are going to receive, is better than the price that they are going to pay for it.

So start paying attention to, what is it that makes you buy. What is the message that goes through your head when you actually make a purchase?

The second piece of advice that I heard when I first started online was, "If you want to be a very good copyrighter, what really all that matters is the headline. And if you get the headline right or wrong, that will determine everything for you.

And so what you need to do is when you are coming up with your sales letter, or your Webinar, or however you are going to deliver your sales message, you need to come up with a great headline. And what you should do is sit down and come up with 100 different headlines, and then go through those and pick out the very best one."

Here's the problem with that: If you are like me, I have a hard enough time coming up with just 1 headline, let alone writing 100 different headlines. And once I get a whole sheet of headlines, even if I could come up with 10-15 different headlines, how the heck would I know which one was the best anyway?

I have no clue! It's just me trying to figure out how to write this thing called a headline, someone told me I had to have. I have no experience about what was the best headline, or which one I should choose. And so that kept me from moving forward for a very long time. In fact it just hindered me from moving forward because then what they told me was "If you can't write a good headline, you need to go to all of the products you can think of, all different websites, and start reading headlines."

Do you know what that did for me? First of all, it overwhelmed me, because I went to all different pages, trying to figure out why it was a good headline, and I had no clue if I was looking at a good headline or not. And then I ended up buying a whole bunch more products because I was reading a whole bunch of other sales pages. Then I was offered a whole bunch of other directions again, forgetting that the whole purpose why I was reading the sales letters, was to write all my headlines, so that I could get my product online to sell.

And don't get me wrong. I do think that a headline is an important part of your sales letter. In fact, the reason why they say the headline is the most important part of your sales letter is because, what's the first thing that people read? If they glance at your headline and are not interested and leave, well, they are not going to buy your product.

What is really important about your headline is that it speaks to your specific avatar, if you will, that it speaks to the right people. Where I used to get hung up, and I see a lot of other people getting hung up with headlines is because it's the most important part of my sales page, or my sales message, I would try to write them for everybody.

I wouldn't try to exclude people. I wouldn't try to talk to my avatar, or my perfect targeted prospect, I would try to talk to everybody. Because that's sort of what I interpreted from what people said about writing all these headlines.

Instead of trying to write 100 headlines, or build up a huge Swipe File, what I would suggest that you do, and this is probably the go-to headlines that Robert and I always start with on most of our sales letters now is, "Who else wants to [Blank], [Blank], and [Blank]?"

And if you start with just that, and I mean it might sound simple, but it is telling people, remember what we talked about in the last section, What makes you buy? What benefit am I going to get if I buy something?

If you can put that into your headline, now it will tie together your whole sales message and it will appeal to the right person. Think about this. Who else wants to [get online fast], [increase conversions], and [manage it all in one place]? Pretty simple right?

So if you can just come up with your headline as "Who else wants to [Three things]" that your product or service will give them, does a couple of things.

First of all, it tells them what benefits they are going to get right off the bat which is what we just talked about, what makes you buy. The second thing is, it makes sure only your targeted audience will move forward with it. And the third thing is, it puts a really clear and concise benefit of what your entire message product will do for somebody right off of the bat.

So don't worry about writing hundreds of headlines, get one down on paper that actually speaks to your targeted audience. And then once you have that in place, and it's actually getting traffic and making sales, you can do this thing called "split testing."

We are not going to go into split testing. But basically what that means is you have the original headline, you have a new headline, and you figure out which one causes people to buy more.

There are some great tools for that, that are free. You can use Google Analytics, it has a great split tester built in, you basically make two separate web pages, put some code on it, and they will keep track of it, and tell you which one is converting better.

You don't need to buy huge copywriting courses, or learn all this theory, or learn all these hypnotic patterns, you just need to start paying attention to what it is that makes you purchase something.

The second thing is you don't need to write hundreds of headlines. You just need to come up with something simple that is good enough. The one that we always start with seems to be "Who else wants to [three things/benefits that they will get out of our product].

The third piece of advice that really held me up, and it's one of the things that I thought I had to have was these great things called "bullet points." And if you look on most sales letters today, on Webinars, on long/short sales letters, you will see that bullet points make up a majority of these sales letters.

What people told me when I was first getting started is "What you need to do Lance is get a bunch of 3x5 note cards. And you need to write a whole bunch of bullet points on them, and then you will have this thing again called Swipe File."

When you want to write out a bullet point you got to all of these note cards and you find one that you like.

What I found was I ended up with a big stack of cards that I never looked at, and never used them again. Wouldn't know why one of them was good, bad, indifferent, or whether it would work or not.

Now here's the solution. I'm going to give you everything you need to know about bullet points right now. The solution on how to write a good bullet point is that you focus on the benefits, again the same message we have been talking about the whole time, the benefits, and not the features of your product.

A benefit of your product is, well, you get online fast. You increase conversions. You can manage your sales letter in one place.

A feature is something like: it is a WordPress plug-in. It has a 50 page manual. It has four built in headlines. Right? Those are features, not benefits.

And if you think about it, the key to writing a good bullet point is being able to, cause most people will start with a feature. They will say "What's interesting about your product?" "The cool thing about my product is, it has a 4 minute training video along with it." Right?

But here is how you go from that feature, which is the 4 minute training video into a benefit. You say: "My bullet point is it has a 4 minute training video." Then, this is something genius I learned from Robert Plank, you start with "Well so what?"

"What do you mean so what? It's a cool video, you get 4 minutes." And I ask the question "Well so what?" And then you say "Well so what, it means that you can get in just the next 4 minutes and be an expert at using it."

Well now that's totally different right? Because now my bullet point went from "I got a 4 minute training video" to "You can have expert knowledge in how to have a sales letter online in JUST 4 minutes." That's the benefit.

What you really want to focus on in writing your bullet points is, what is the result that somebody is going to get, again, the back to what makes you buy, what makes a good headline, what is the result that somebody is going to get. Not how it is delivered. Not what it is, but what it will give the person that actually buys it, if they go through the what it is.

And so if you stay away from those three things. Don't worry about the huge copywriting courses right now, just think about what makes you buy. You don't need to write tons and tons of headlines, start with the simple one that gives them the three benefits. And don't worry about these huge bullet points. You will be on your way to getting your copy online and ready in the record time.

It's important that we take that even one step further, and talk about really how it is that you need to structure your sales, and what you need to say in order to actually convince somebody that the benefit that they are going to get out ways the monetary cost of what it is that they are going to get.

I believe that this can be broken down into 5 simple questions. And if you answer these 5 simple questions, and you can even do this in order of the way that they are coming out, first of all it gives you a clear and concise template of what to say inside your sales letters/process/presentations, but it also gives you this clear cut what it is to say.

Here are the questions are that you need to answer. If you can answer these 5 questions in order, and think about as I'm telling you what they are, you will find that your sales material will be easier to write and will convert a lot higher.

Here they are:

1.   Why is it important?
2.   What is it?
3.   How is it delivered?
4.   What am I going to get?
5.   How much is it?

That's it! If you can answer those 5 questions in that order, you will have much better sales copy. Let's walk through them. I think this is going to make a lot of sense to you.

The 1st question is: why is it important? And if you want to think of this as your opening story, if you will, for your sales copy. Why is it important to the person coming to the website?

For example: at Paper Template which is a WordPress plug-in that sort of lays out all of your sales copy, gives you a Swipe File, basically a copywriting course all built into one.

The sales letter starts with "If you have ever tried to setup your own sales page or opting page, you have probably experienced the frustration of..." and it lists some technical frustrations. Like: "what HTML editor should I use? How should I make things look the right way? How do I get images in the right place? How do I make Buy buttons?" And all this other stuff.

A bunch of technical details. So why is it important? If you have tried to setup a sales page, or an opting page, you probably know that one of the big frustrations is the technical stuff.

And then it goes into, once you get over the technical issues, then you are suddenly faced with questions like: What do I write on my page? Right?

Right off the bat, the story is, if you are having these kinds of problems, well, our ideal person that is comes to this page is having these problems. So we list out the problems, which is the opening story, why is it important? If you have had all of this stuff before, well great! Because I got a solution that will answer all of those problems that we have just laid out.

Why is it important? What is it that is stopping me from getting the results that I want? And this works in any niche, whether it's weight-loss. So if you have said if you have ever tried to lose weight, you know that it's hard to find good things that you actually like to eat. It's hard to find exercise regiments that are fun and simple to do, it's hard to count calories, whatever it is.

But what you need to do is sort of tell that story that your prospect is going through, and talk about what things they have probably tried. But more importantly setting up the actual benefit that somebody is going to get. It's all the things that your product solves.

Then you get to the second session, that is, what is it? Now this doesn't have to be anymore than saying "I have just laid out why this is important, these are probably the things that you have tried before that don't work, these are the things that have frustrated you, about whatever your solution is." And then very simply all you have to do in the what is it, is say "Introducing [Whatever your product is]."

And then lay out, if it's a course, what those modules are. If it is a WordPress plug-in, what that plug-in is and how it works. If it is a good or a service, what it is you provide somebody. So that they know, well here is the problems that I have definitely experienced, or the problems that I will run into. Now what is it exactly.

Think about your psychology when you buy something, I mean what do you want to know? What does this thing solve for me, and what is it? Very simple thing, and then when you tell them what it is. So "Introducing [Your product]. And here's why it's different [Blank]. Here is how it solves those things [Blank]." You tell them how the product is delivered.

Now this is something really important, it's something you see so many people miss over. This is the what of it right? This is the "ok, I get that I have a problem that you can solve. I know what it is, I know it's a product called the Paper Template, or a weight-loss product called 'How to Lose Weight,' or a cartoon drawing product called 'How to Draw Cartoons. Now I want to know how is it delivered?"

"Is it mailed to my house? Is it an email? Is it an e-course, a video, is it a report, what is it?" Because that's the next question in my mind, is it what I'm looking for? Does it solve my problem? Now, what is it?

And so, all you do is tell them exactly how it is delivered. We like to do in basically a table that says is it 4 modules, here's what the modules are, is it videos, whatever it is. But tell them how it is delivered.

Then what you need to do is you need to summarize everything up. So again you need to tell them what they are going to get. But this time, what you want to do is tell them the results, and you want to give what we like to call the 'stack.'

Basically what you can think of the stack as a one sheet, it's the summary of everything you are going to buy. And the best analogy that probably everyone of you guys have seen before, is if you go in to buy a new automobile, or you go to a car dealership. What's on the window of every single car on the lot? If you walk around there is a sheet of paper that says what the model is, what year it is, what kind of radio does it have, what kind of locks does it have, what kind of interior, what kind of brakes, all of the information with prices next to it. And then how much all of those add up to. And then the price that you are going to pay.

And it's the exact same thing with your sales process. You have told somebody why it's important to them, what problem you are going to solve, you have told what you are going to solve with your solution, the what is it, you told them how it was delivered, whether that's with modules, videos, training, report, or whatever it was.

Now you need to summarize all of that by telling them again "here is the result that you are going to get, you are going to be able to lose weight finally, once and for all, get rid of yo-yo dieting, write sales letters with this one easy WordPress plug-in, really simply now." Whatever that result is, plus the stack, or the summary offer which is each portion of it listed out with the price that is associated with it.

Once you have done that, the only thing that is left for you to put into that sales process, or into that sales message is to put how much does it actually cost. Then you just put the Buy button and the actual price.

If you think about it, if you follow this process, it takes you through the natural progression of what you think of and what your prospect thinks of what's important to them when you go through the buying process.

"Why is this thing important to me and what's it going to solve for me? Ok. I'm interested, I have that problem. I would like to overcome my issue that you have laid out for me. Now what is it? OH! You have a training course that helps me learn how to finally lose weight once and for all! Well that's great, I'm interested in it. How is it delivered? Oh cool! It's DVDs that are going to get mailed to my door. So I know exactly what to expect after I hit the buy button. All right, now what am I getting again? Oh I'm going to finally get off the yo-yo dieting plan. And now I can see it all listed out. I'm going to get DVDs mailed to my door. I'm going to get an instant access to a report today, there's a tool inside the members area. How much does it actually cost? Perfect! That has more value than what this cost is. I will go ahead and buy that, right now."

If you think of your sales process just like that, the natural progression, translate that into your sales copy, you are going to start making more sales, see higher conversions, and you are going to see less refunds because people will actually know what it is that they are getting into, and what they are buying, right off of the bat.

And you can get all of this built into templates, built into layouts, with push buttons, click buttons solutions for your WordPress sites at papertemplate.com

Add these into your daily copywriting and sales routines and watch your conversions sky rocket!

Step 6: Sales Letter

Now you want to setup your sales letter. Remember, we had originally setup our opt-in page at our root URL like membershipcube.com. When you got your sales letter ready, you put this at the root and move this to a subfolder, /free or /gift. Inside of Income Machine, you guys use Paper Template, all you have to do is click a button. You just say, this is no longer the front page, this is the front page and it'll automatically switch all of that for you so you don't even have to think about it.

The important part about the sales letter, when you write your copy, again when we see how we talk about the webinar courses and how to set it up, your sales copy will write itself. Again, all you have to know about sales copywriting is when somebody says they want to know what it's going to do for them, the headline is "Are you even interested in it? Am I in the right place?" Then, what it is going to do for me? What am I going to get if I actually buy or purchase your course? How is it delivered? Is it something I'm going to get instant access to, is it dripped out, is it DVDs that are going to get mailed for me and then, how much does it cost?

That's it. If you do those 4 things on your sales letter, that's all that you need. You all guys have access to Paper Template. The cool thing is that if you use that, you go in there and there's a pre-written part and this is already all laid out for you. It's literally fill in the blanks. There's 80 headlines, you can just pick one you like, fill in the blanks, thoughts that are missing and it goes through, like tell me why it's important.

We do what's called an offer stack. Answer the question of, "What is it? How am I going to get it?" and then there's a Buy button. Really, you don't have to do much more than if you setup your products the way we're going to talk about in the next section.

We have what we call the offer stack. If you look on all of our sales pages at the bottom, there'll be a yellow area, it's like table. You'll see this in our webinars too where it'll be like "You get module 1 and it's worth 497" We say

So many people go wrong in their copy. They say, "What you're going to get is a 10 hour video and a 497 page e-book" You can't win when you play that game. First of all, nobody cares. What do you care about when you're buying a product? You don't care how many hours it is, you don't care how many pages it is, you care what result you're going to get after you buy it.

I could care less if it's 5 pages or 600 pages if they get me to the same result. In fact, what I want is the 5 page one because I get it faster. I'm probably willing to pay more for the 5 page one than I am for the 600 page one if they promise to get me to the same result, and they actually do. That's why when we say it's an offer stack, we tell them what they're going to get meaning, in Module 1, you're going to learn how to make your income machine or what's involved. In Module 2 you're going to learn how to sell on a sales letter.

What they care is what they're going to get at the end. Think about that in your products too. We're going to talk about this in the next section. Nobody cares how long it is. You can't win that game. You can't win by telling somebody... If you tell somebody it's 10 minutes, somebody's going to look at it and go: "Damn, it can't be that good. It's only 10 minutes long." But if you say it's an hour, somebody's going to look at it and go: "It's going to take them an hour to teach me that? It must suck. It's filled with fluff."

All anybody cares about is the end result. You can't win with telling numbers, you can't win with a template. The only way that you can win with everybody is telling them what result they're going to get after taking your product or course.

Time to Rethink Your Business

Hey everybody, Lance Tamashiro here, and today I want to talk to you about why you need to be thinking about having a recurring income for your online business. Now, a lot of people that I know and that I've worked with in the past think, "I'm just going to work really, really hard on this one cool e-book, I'm going price it at $7 dollars and everybody in the world is going to come buy it, and I'll just be rich!" The truth is that's not the case. The whole key on making money on the Internet is to build a recurring income.

The Key to Long Term Income

Now, that's the big point here. Everything else that you do is just spinning your wheels, if you're not thinking of making a recurring income then all that you're really doing is doing the same thing that you're doing in your day job, you're trading your time for dollars, and what you really want to do is get to the point where you basically put up a membership site, get something that's recurring and get paid for it over and over again.

Niche Is Not Important

Now, the one thing that I really want to stress to everybody here is that your niche is not important. Now, a lot of people think, well, I can only make recurring income in internet marketing, I can only make income trying to teach people how to play the guitar, that's not the truth! The truth is, is that if you have anything at all to teach or a service to give, then, you can start your own membership site.

Every Successful Business Is Based On "Memberships"

How do I know this? Well, look around you! Every single business model that is successful both online and offline is based around a membership model. I want you to change the way you think about memberships right now, today!

A membership is not just something where you get new content every month. Its something where you get to bill people every month either for your information or your service, and let me give you a couple of examples, I bet the majority of you have a cellphone. Guess what? That is a membership site, they have a fix term length, usually it's like two years and you have to pay over and over and over again. Guess what I bet you most of you have landline service if you don't have a cell phone service. That too is a form of a recurring membership site.

Do you own a car? I bet you make car payments. Do you own a house? Or pay rent? All of those are types of membership sites, and all examples of things that you can do to trade your time for dollars that are recurring instead of one to one, you want to look at this as one to many.

Building A Membership Site Is Not Hard!

I've recently pulled my list and the big thing that I found is that people thought, well Lance this is way too hard! It's way too hard to setup a recurring membership site, its way to hard to get people to pay me time and time again for my information and I want to tell you right now, that's false! You need to change the way you're thinking about this.

I know what you're thinking... Lance, I don't have any content. Am I an expert in anything? How am I going to get people to pay me over and over and over again? Well the truth is that if you know anything at all, then you're an expert.

One of the big things, especially in the Internet marketing industry that people forget is that there is a huge learning curve. So, even if you just know how to put up a squeeze page, even if you know just how setup an autoresponder, even if you just know a good program, an affiliate program to promote, all of those are information that somebody just getting started doesn't know that you had to learn and that's enough information that makes you an expert on somebody, and that's the key to learning more and more and being able to charge more and more for your membership site.

It's Not Too Technical!

The second thing that people told me is that it's way too technical to setup a membership site. Again, false! All you need to know is WordPress, you need to have the right plug-ins and you need to have the right scripts. This is cheap, this is easy to do, and it's not hard at all. Even if you just re-think your model and rethink of your autoresponder as a membership, then guess what? You have the ability to make a recurring income and a membership site.

I want you to stop overthinking this! It is true, the key to a successful online business or business in the offline world is recurring income but it doesn't have to be as hard as you're making it. You don't need fancy scripts. You don't need a ton of information.

You Only Need To Be One Step Ahead

All you need to do is to start at the point where you're at, whether it's beginning guitar. Remember, if you're learning guitar, you know something more than somebody that is just getting started, and you have something to teach that person. You don't have to fill-up an entire membership site for years and years when you don't even have a member, and that is something that is really, really bothers me. The truth is you only have to be one step ahead of your first member.

If you have a membership site, why would you spend a year building up content when you don't even have somebody paying you yet? Wouldn't it be a better idea to make weeks' worth of content, find that first member and always stay one day, or one week, or one month ahead of that one person? It's been told on the Internet that the average lifespan of a membership site is two to four months, so let's round it up and call it three months.

If the average time that somebody stays in a membership is only three months why are so many of you spending months and months and months building six months, one year, two years of content? All you need to do is stay one step ahead of your longest subscriber. In that way you're not spinning your wheels. You can start bringing in money while you're increasing your own knowledge and starting to bring money into your online business

A couple of weeks ago I was with my friend Robert Plank, hanging out in North Carolina, and had a discussion where we about, "What is a membership site?" What constitutes a membership site? What "officially makes it" so that I have a membership site, and you want to know what we came up with? It's that all of these big terms that people are throwing around are untrue.

The only thing that you need to have a membership site is to charge one person one payment or more, and that makes it a membership site. It can be fixed term, it can be open ended, but think about the example like I gave you earlier. You have a car payment, you know exactly how many payments you're going to have to make until that membership ends and you own the car. If you have an e-book that you sell for $97, guess what if you're having trouble selling it at $97, make it two payments of $47 and suddenly you have a membership site. So, stop over thinking it, but I want to know do you have a membership site?

What is your membership site? If you think you have any sort of product at all, you have a membership site, and another thing that I want to tell you is that I personally own a membership site that is made completely of other people's products. That's right, I took master resell rights, private label rights, and different types of products, threw them up all on a single website and I charge people month after month after month to get access to these. So, without even owning your own product, you can successfully start your own membership site.

One of the most important things that you need to know about your membership site is what is that retention rate? And how long do people stay in, and it's sort of like what I was talking about earlier, what is the purpose of having a hundred days' worth of content, if you only keep people on average for 30 days? You've just wasted 70 days' worth of time, of content that people would never see.

Wouldn't it be better to restructure that content so that you can build over and over and over, or stretch it out so that you can only have content for the amount of time that people are going to see it?

The main point that I'm driving home here is that there's lots and lots or easy solutions! In fact Robert Plank and I have six proven models that we use over and over again to build recurring income, and most people just think of us as like these "Products Creators" that's people that are always pimping out new things but the truth is, is that we try to put everything we can into a recurring income because we would rather do the work once and get paid for it many times, than do the work once and get paid for it once, and that's what I want to encourage you to do.

Step 7: Membership Site

That's the sales letter part and then, everything for us is delivered inside of the membership site. For us, membership site doesn't mean it goes on forever, it means that it takes the orders for us, it lets the people in for us, it cancels them if they quit paying us and it handles their username and password if they use it. It's our virtual assistant, it handles everything for us as far as payment collection and product delivery.

We use Wishlist Member, which has been fantastic for us and we use PayPal. All of this stuff that people talk about, "Can't use PayPal, can't do any of this, they'll shut you off" Those people are all probably people that were doing shady stuff. If you're selling a legitimate product, you're not getting a huge refund rate... You're going to get refund, that's just the name of the game online but if you don't have a huge refund rate, PayPal doesn't care at all, they love you.

The one thing that we do, I don't do it as much now but when we were first getting started and our accounts were new at PayPal, before every single launch for a while I would just call them every week just to say: "Hey, this is Lance. This is our account. Are there any issues?" or "Hey, this is Lance. We're going to be launching on Wednesday a $9.97 product. We're expecting X number of sales, just wanted to let you know. Please call me if there's an issue. Can you put this on my account that I called."

In almost 4 years now, a lot of money through that account, never had one problem withdrawing, never had one problem with them freezing our funds, never had any problems at all. The only time we did have a problem is, I think we were trying to refund somebody $1,000 because they were just a problem, they kept rebuying, we kept refunding them and PayPal called me and said: "I don't know what to do but this guy keeps saying you keep refunding his $1,000 and you won't take it. What's going on?" We were like: "Can you block him so he doesn't buy?" They were like: "We've never had anybody call to complain to us that a merchant wouldn't take their money but I guess we can stop this."

They will call, they have my cell phone number, I have it marked so when it calls that I know it's PayPal. They've called us maybe once or twice just to check on a transaction or look at something but if you build that relationship with them, you won't have a problem. Just let them know what you're selling, don't try to hide anything from them. We used to ask them if our sales pages were okay. We were totally transparent. We'd never had a single issue with them.

That's all we've ever used. I'll call PayPal and say: "Here's our sales page. This is what we're selling. Is there a problem?" They'll tell you. Every time, after you talk to them, tell them to put a note on your account that you called and talked to so and so and what it was, they'll keep that history there. That way, when they see you reaching out like that, if a problem does arise, their default isn't to shut you off and freeze your funds, their default is to call and talk to you because you've proven that you're not hiding from them, you're not doing anything shady, you're trying to talk to them. We're going to talk more about membership sites this afternoon as well.

If you see anything that looks weird on your account or just a big number of sales are coming in, just call them and touch base, you won't have any problems with them.

Four Membership Site Myths

We've been having a discussion about what you need to actually build a membership site, how to build content, how to technically overcome some of the barriers that a lot of you are having producing your membership sites.

I don't blog very often, but I felt that this was a needed conversation. What I see happening in the marketplace is a lot of the "gurus" are basically telling you things about memberships when

a) They might not even have very many of their own

b) I really feel like they're doing a lot of the "teaching" that they're doing with ulterior motives.

I've heard a lot of common themes, and I want to squash the problems that you guys perceived that you're having with creating your own memberships sites – because as we all know, most of us came online in order to earn a passive, recurring income and that obviously translates into a membership site, but what happens is that we find ourselves working even more than we did at a lower hourly rate than we did at our day jobs and you're never going to get ahead that way.

I want to discuss with you today are the "membership site myths" that your favorite "guru" wants you to believe.

WARNING!

I want to start off with a very basic warning, and the warning is this – that this blog post is only for people who want the absolute truth.

If you follow me at all, if you read my emails, if you read my blog posts, you know that I'm not one to sugarcoat things, and when I see a problem in the marketplace, I like to talk about it.

So, why do you want a membership site anyway?

The reason why I wanted a membership site and based on the feedback that you've given me is that you wanted to work less, you want to earn more, and basically you want to enjoy life.

Just to give you a real quick example, my partner, Robert Plank and I, currently have over 20 membership sites up and running. Yes, that's 20 that we've created in less than a year, there's probably even more than that at this point now, but these membership sites bring us in over $20,000 per month passively. And when I say passively, we maybe put 30 minutes to 60 minutes per month of work into it. So, not a bad trade-off. If you ask me, it's a great hourly rate, and one of the things that it lets us do is enjoy life.

Just recently, we happened to be at a conference in Las Vegas and we were having a discussion, and Robert says to me,

"Hey Lance, it's your birthday. I want to take you, your wife, your child, Grace, who is a very cute little girl, I might add, and his girlfriend, Sarah – to Hawaii."

So, that night we got on the internet, he booked us first class tickets to Hawaii, went there for about 5 days. In fact, we're big LOST fans. So, he took us on this all-day tour of LOST.

While we did that, our money kept coming in and we didn't do any work. No work whatsoever. We just relaxed, enjoyed, recuperated. And the reason we were able to do that is because we have the correct setups in membership site, and what we want to do is show you how to do that as well.

The cool thing about this, like I was saying, is it all happened on autopilot. We didn't even answer emails, log in to the internet, nothing while we were way at Hawaii.

Myth #1 - Use Free Software

I'm seeing this more and more and more over the internet is that "Free software and free membership site setups are good."

Let me just get this right out of the way.

The argument that these "gurus" are teaching is that you should start with a free setup solution because you can upgrade later.

But let me ask you a question, how many PLR or Resale Rights Products have you bought?

And of those, how many have you actually setup online?

How many sales pages have you said that you're going to go back and edit and make better?

How many products have you created that you said you're going to go back and update?

My guess is, if you're anything like me, you've got lots of this stuff and the truth is you never went back and upgraded.

The Truth Is This NEVER Happens

We're so bombarded with moving our businesses forward that we never go back to do any, to go back and "fix" anything. So, why not just get it right the first time?

Wouldn't it be better to start with a solid foundation that you can grow with instead of trying to worry about the headache of how to change your whole system?

What they never tell you is that it's next to impossible to migrate your setup. They tell you to put it on all of this free software, they tell you that you can go back at any time once you've started to build an income and you can migrate that over.

The truth is it's near impossible to do that.

Also, what happens if you need support?

Do you really think that the author of a "free plugin" is going to be really worried about helping you if you have a problem with their software?

Personally, I would much rather go with a big company who has a staff that's dedicated to answering my problems when I have one.

Myth #2 - "I'm Not An Expert"

I hear this over and over, and this was probably the biggest common theme that I heard from the emails that you guys have sent me.

"I'm not an expert. Who will listen to me? How do I get people to pay for the stuff that I want to know?"

"Who will pay for my information?"

Here's A Little Secret

This is actually an overwhelmed tactics that the "gurus" want you to believe.

Why would they want you to believe this?

Why would they want you to believe that you don't have enough information to become an expert? That you don't know enough in order to teach somebody else what it is that you know?

Well, it's really simple. If they can keep making you believe that you're not an expert, then you have to keep buying their products. Think about that for a minute. It makes absolute sense, and if you actually step back and think about the people that are telling you to setup memberships sites, that are telling you to find a niche, and then they're saying you don't know enough, it's a tactic that they want you to believe.

The truth is, is that the majority of people online are looking for facts, concise information. Can you find out everything about membership sites or everything about your niche online for free?

The answer, honestly is probably, but what people pay for is that consolidated, concise, no-fluff information.

I don't care what niche you're in, there is always a newbie or somebody that knows less than you that you can pass that information onto. For example, I got started in internet marketing as a list builder. Now, are there people out there that sell products everyday on how to build 10,000-person list? How to build 100,000-person list?

Yes.

I couldn't do that. What I did was I used my results.

What I learned how to do was build a list of 137 people, and I sold that product. That product sold like crazy.

Why? Because there were people who didn't even know how to do what I knew how to do So, I could take them, and as I learned new things, I had continuing information to teach to them.

Think about that for a minute. You are an expert to somebody and the truth is is that there's many, many more beginners on the internet in every single niche than there are experts. There's very few "experts."

If you feel like you know more than somebody about your hobby, your passion, your niche, as you should, then it's very easy to market towards people who know less than you. And as they learn more, you are going to be learning more as well.

Don't think that you're not an expert. Every single one of you, are and I've yet to meet any of the students that we have anywhere from $300 students to $1000 coaching clients that have come to us and not felt like they were an expert after our training – because the truth is it's just a mindset shift. Once you understand what's happening to you in the marketplace, it makes it very easy to see that you actually are an expert.

Myth #3 - "I Can't Generate Enough Content"

This one drives me absolutely crazy – because the biggest reason that people fail online with membership sites is because they think they have this one big idea.

They think they have this one membership site that is going to basically be their ticket out. So what do they do?

Well, they try to create years and years and years worth of content upfront before they even launch it, and this makes no sense to me.

Let's think about this for a minute. Why would you spend your time creating 4 months, 6 months, 1 year, 2 years worth of content when you don't even have a subscriber yet?

Nobody is going to see that for 6 months, 2 years. So what Robert and I do is when we actually create membership sites, we're always just staying one step ahead of our longest subscribers.

Re-Think Your Idea Of A Membership

First of all, I want you to think about a fixed-term membership site. Most of the membership sites that I run are what we call fixed-term, which means that it starts at one point and has a definite end point. If there is 6 months worth of content, they pay for 6 months, and at the end of 6 months, they have lifetime to access to all the updates, all the information, anything else that we might add/change along the way.

The point is you've now moved from something open-ended, which most people, let's face it, are afraid of pain. If somebody told you you're going to pay $47 for the rest of your life or you're going to pay $47 every 2 weeks for the next 8 months, there's a big difference in there. You can actually see the end, you can see what's happening, and it's a much easier sell that way.

The cool thing is, is you only have to be one step ahead of your longest subscriber.

Now, this is a huge mindset shift for you and what you've probably been taught about membership sites. I know it was for me because when I got started, I thought the same way – I needed a membership site that would last forever. The truth is, is that you don't know if there's a market for it, you don't know if people are going to like your content.

If you create 2 years worth of stuff to go in your membership site, you won't even know people are going to like the content that you're creating and you don't have time to course-correct. What we like to teach you to do is to actually just be 1 week, 2 weeks, maybe a month ahead of your earliest subscriber, so that

A) you're not creating content that nobody's going to like

B) you can course-correct as you go along.

If people need different information than you think because you're going to get feedback, then you can adjust as you go

You also know where people are dropping off. So, you don't end up with a bunch of empty content that you can't use.

So, can you create enough content? Yes, you can, as long as you can shift your mindset and think a little bit differently about your membership site.

Myth #4 - "I'm Not A Techie"

Basically, people think they don't have the technical expertise in order to build a membership site. Again, this is something that your "guru" wants you to believe. Now, why would they want you to believe this? Very simple again – because they have a vested interested in you thinking that, so that you can buy their training, so that they can encourage you to stick with them and continue to buy their products.

All You Need To Know

You need to know how to setup a website, you need to know how to manage your members, you need to know how to handle payments. And by the way, most of the free solutions on the market don't do all these, which actually means you spend your time working on these things rather than enjoying your life. This is why I personally believe the free models suck. It's too much technical work.

In reality, all that you need to build a successful numerous number of membership sites is WordPress – that's 100% free product that comes with almost all hosting accounts. If not, you can get it at WordPress.org. Super easy to install, you just click a button, and it's all done for you.

You need Wishlist Member. Why do I like to promote wish list member and encourage you to use it?

A) it's what I use for all of my sites

B) I know that they are a giant company, I know the owners of it, and I know that they have awesome technical support, and they're always updating with the new versions of WordPress that are coming out and enhancing their features. By the way, you don't get that with free solutions. They have a vested interest in beating things like WordPress upgrades to market.

The third thing that you need is a plugin that Robert Plank wrote, called WordPress Drip. This is a little bit more expensive. It sells for ~~$2,495.00~~ $47.

However, if you're a member of Membership Cube, then it comes for free along with your Wishlist Member license and all of the training that you need to get up and started right away.

The cool thing is just knowing these three pieces of software that you need, you can have your membership site up and running today. Literally today, you can have a membership site up and running, and spend your time marketing your site rather than spending your time trying to generate all of your content.

I want to thank you for taking a couple minutes out of your day to talk about these "membership site myths" with you. I hope that I've expanded your mind and helped you understand what actually happening in the marketplace.

I would really appreciate it if you go down to the bottom of the page right now, fill out a comment, let me know what your thoughts are.

Step 8: Traffic

Finally, traffic. What's awesome is, when you have all this setup, what it start to look like, back to here, you've got your opt-in page, you've got your sale page, you've got your blog, you've got your membership site and you're webhosting all setup, now your blog is the first piece of your traffic, now you can just start plugging in whatever that is, whether it's going to be paid, whether it's going to be joint venture, whether it's going to be a book and it all plugs in, and your whole system is now setup in place where you don't have to mess with anything. Can you go back and make it better? Sure, if you want.

You don't have to be in the state of chicken and the egg, state of: "I can't do that because that's not ready.", state of: "My sales page isn't quite ready" It is, if you use the template, it's good enough. Especially if you launch the way that we're going to suggest that you launch, you don't even really need a sales page, to be honest but what's cool is the other piece here that you're building that's not on here is your autoresponder. No matter what anybody says to you, this is your best traffic, always.

They are people that know you, they are people that have a connection with you and it's on demand, any time that you want it. You start to build this traffic back to here, your leads and offers. Now, you can send this wherever you want, to any product that you've got, to any offer that you might have. Again, this allows you, once you have it setup this way with these things... We walk you through in Income Machine, what you guys all have full access to exactly how did we setup a real life site, real time with you so every single piece is setup and you can have that there.

This is literally what we do for every one of our offers. What's neat is you can scale any piece of this. I can make as many opt-in pages as I want, as many sales pages, as many offers and in all this traffic just depends on where I funnel it to and what I want to use up my autoresponder.

Affiliate Programs & Retargeting

Today, what I want to do is give you some real world strategies that you can start using in your business today, to start getting you more traffic to your website. I work with entrepreneurs from all over the world and hands down the number one complaint, no matter whether they're just starting out, whether they've been around for a while or whether they're making 6-7 figures a year, they all have the same question, the same problem, the same complaint. And that is "How do I get more converting traffic to my website?" That's exactly what we're going to talk about today.

What I really hope that you get out of today's episode, besides some really good strategies to implement, is a mindset shift. And here is what I mean. Maybe you're like me. When I got started online, what I was looking for was: well, I knew I needed targeted traffic to my website. Because if I could get some traffic, that meant I'll be able to get some sales hopefully. And you might have fallen into this trap that I know that I did. When I went out looking for ways to get traffic to my website, I wanted traffic for more preferably free. I was looking for free ways where I can get traffic to my website. I would do things like write articles, I would make blog posts, I would join these things called JV Giveaway Events. I even did a little bit of this thing called ad-swapping, where people with mailing lists would mail to my offer and I would mail to their offer in return. All of these ways of getting free traffic.

Does free traffic work and should you use some of these strategies - notice that I said some of these strategies - for your business? I think the answer is definitely you should. The problem with strategies like article marketing or writing blog posts or doing YouTube videos is - they're hit-or-miss, right? Because you don't know which articles are going to rank high inside of different search engines. You don't know which videos are going to rank well within places like YouTube. And yeah, tricks come around every once in a while, where people can show you how to rank really easily with a search engine or rank a video really quickly with YouTube. But what's wrong with those strategies? Well they always get closed down, right? They're based on loopholes, they're not based on real business practices.

The other problem is that when you rely on most of these types of free traffic sources, you're at the mercy of the search engines. And I mean you guys probably have heard this all of the time where Google would come out and change their algorithms and suddenly real businesses, scam businesses, high quality businesses, low quality businesses are all the same, are literally blown away overnight out of the Google search engines. And businesses are literally lost in just a whim for what Google thinks.

I don't like to have my business rely on things like what the search engine thinks is good today or whether YouTube thinks my video should rank well. Although I do think that you should have those types of pieces, as a long term strategy in your business.

One thing that really changed my mindset about advertising was this thing called actually paying for advertising. I want you to think about something really quick. What does it cost for traditional big successful offline companies and even some online companies to advertise on Network TV? It costs like a million dollars to run an ad spot during the Super Bowl. It's not cheap to run these infomercials on television, it's not cheap to run the same Pepsi or Coca Cola commercial over and over again every single time you turn on the television.

I ask you: why do these companies do this? Well my guess is that the reason why companies spend this crazy amount of money on advertising online and offline - I just used television as an example - is because they know they're getting a return on their investment for it. So if somebody's spending a million dollars on a Super Bowl commercial, they already know from their testing and from their numbers that they know how normal commercials are going to convert, that they're going to earn their money back on that.

Think about what this might do for your online business. Think about if instead of always searching for the cheapest traffic, 1 cent per click or 10 cents per click or whatever that is, that you actually switched your mindset and said how much revenue can I generate per click? Would that not change your entire business model? I mean for example if you were selling a 1,000 dollar product, why are you out there looking for 1 cent clicks? Why are you out there looking for 10 cent clicks and then wondering why that traffic is not converting or why it's not working for you.

I'm not saying that you shouldn't be striving to decrease your advertising cost. What I am saying though is that does it make sense if you spend 500 dollars on advertising to sell a 1,000 dollar product, is that worth it? And my answer is: Yeah, of course it is. You've spent 500 dollars, say you spent 10 dollars per click, generating 50 clicks back to your 1,000 dollar product and you sold one of them. Was that worth your advertising? Well, yeah, you made back all of your money, you doubled your money, right? You spent 500 plus you've got 500 in revenue.

What I see a lot of people doing - and I've been guilty of this as well - is I will seek out all of the cheapest advertising places I can find. I mean I even probably have done searches - well I have done searching like this on the Internet - where I looked for cheap advertising on the Internet, low cost advertising for my website, things like that, without even thinking what I am willing to spend for the traffic actually to convert.

Now hopefully that changes the way that you're looking at some of these. And again, I'm not suggesting that you should spend on the most expensive traffic. What I'm suggesting is that wouldn't it be worth it to spend a little bit more on your advertising to actually get results?

You need to start tracking how your advertising is working. And this is something that a lot of people put off, because it seems difficult, it seems like a lot of work, it seems really hard to do. But what I'd like to suggest to you is that it's pretty easy to actually track your advertising. One of the methods that we use in our business is a tool called link tracker. And don't worry about writing that down, I'll have it in the show notes for you, so you can go check that up. But basically what link tracker does is it allows me to put in a URL and they give me a clock to link - for lack of a better word - another link that I'm able to use in my advertising that's unique that tells me how many times it was clicked on and how many purchases or opt-ins or whatever action - either a sale or an action - resulted from somebody clicking on that link. And it allows me to very quickly separate out all of my different advertising campaigns.

If I'm advertising Setup An Affiliate program or Backup Creator or WP Import or any of the products that Robert and I sell online, I can simply go to this tool, I can create a unique advertising link and then I can submit that link to Facebook. I can submit another link for Google AdWords. I can submit another link for DirectCPV. Basically I come up with a unique link for each of my advertising sources and from there I can see how many times it was clicked on and how many sales resulted from that traffic source.

Now think about the power if you had a simple tool like this in order for your business to grow. One of the things that Robert and I strive to do to keep our business growing is we try to invest 20% of our revenue into advertising, into bringing more sales in. Now if you're not tracking how that advertising is working for you, you're just throwing away money, right? What we're able to do is to test different advertising methods. We're allowed to see what's working, see what ads are working, see what ad sources are working and then make a decision based on their actual true results and numbers, whether or not that advertising method is working for us.

For example, I know when I first got started, I would do things like: I'm going to set-up a Google AdWords campaign, I'm going to bid 10 cents a click, I'm going to pick a gazillion keywords and I'm going to hope something happens. Literally what happened was I would lose 200 dollars, 1,000 dollars, I might get a sale or two but I wouldn't know what keywords, I wouldn't know if I got a return on the money, I wouldn't know anything other than I spent 1,000 dollars and I didn't get 1,000 dollars back on my return.

Using the tool like keyword tracker really can change your business, because you can now see if what it costs and what you're converting at and you can know exactly how much you can spend on your advertising in order to get a return that makes sense for your business.

Now I want to talk a little bit about some of the different ways that we do advertise and some of the ways that we do generate traffic. I want to talk about first of all one that is a free method and then I want to talk about a couple of different paid methods that you can use.

Now our favorite free method of advertising, hands down, no question about it, that gets us the best results, is always, always, always our affiliate program. And not only our affiliate program, but actually giving our affiliates instant commissions. Here is what I mean. Most affiliate programs work like this: you sign up, you get a link, the affiliate promotes the product however they're going to promote it, they make some sales, they can log in and look at how many sales they've made, how much commissions are coming in and then they have to wait, right? They have to wait 30 days, 60 days, sometimes 90 days. I've got personally an affiliate program I'm waiting to be paid out on that I haven't been paid out on in two and a half years. I don't think that check's coming. But there's still a lot of money in that account that somebody owes me and we'll see if it happens. But those are the frustrations for a lot of affiliates and those are actually things that stop a lot of affiliates from promoting products.

Now what Robert and I like to do is this thing called Instant Commissions. What that means is that rather than the affiliate having to wait for a commission check, like having to wait 30, 60, 90 days in order to get their commissions paid out to them, they're actually paid directly to their PayPal account as soon as the sale is made. Now this is a huge incentive for affiliates, because now if they need some money, they can take an email, they can send it out to their list and they can have money rolling in literally as soon as the email goes out.

This is an amazing technique, because not too many people out there online are doing it and the affiliates love it. Now the neat thing about doing an instant commission affiliate program is you can do different levels of commissions for it. For example, when we launched backupcreator.com, we actually gave away for a limited time 100% instant commissions. Now a lot of people look at that and they say "Well why would you do that? Why would you have a product out there, give away all of the commissions and isn't that what I'm working for? I'm trying to earn all of this money."

But I want you, again, just like your advertising, I wanted you to change the way that you thought about your business. I want you to change the way that you think about your business with this. What I'm going to suggest to you is that by launching our product with 100% commissions - and we literally sent out tens of thousands of dollars in commissions during that launch - what did it do for our business? Well first of all, what it did was it created a huge buzz for our product, right? It created - all the affiliates out there in the world were talking about this product, because they were all earning instant commissions and it was a high converting product.

The marketplace immediately knew what our product was. Immediately was one of those products that everybody's talking about inside of the marketplace. That's number one. Number two is every one of those leads, every one of those people that bought now became leads to our other products. We now captured them as customers, we now had their email addresses, we could now follow up with them for our future products. I would suggest that when you do this, you're building a much better long term asset for your business, because somebody that has bought from you once already is more likely to buy from you a second time. Why? Well because they've done it before, they know what your products quality is like and they know what to expect from you.

Getting over that hurdle of somebody purchasing from you initially, now you have a much higher qualified lead. And here's another thing that people miss about this whole thing, is that we're all on a whole different bunch of marketers' list or we read different blogs or we follow different people on Facebook or Twitter. Whatever that group is that you follow, if one of them recommends a product to you, you are more likely to feel comfortable purchasing that product than if you heard about it called or through an advertising or from somebody you didn't already trust. So that "know, like and trust" factor is automatically given over, transferred from your affiliate to your through their customer, if that makes sense. And you build a much bigger, better asset for your company, to make future sales and build that email list up.

The next thing that I want to talk about to you is advertising on Facebook. If you have not yet started advertising on Facebook, I really encourage you to look into that. Because we shied away from advertising on Facebook for a long, long time. Until a couple of things happened. Until we realized how easy, fast and powerful Facebook advertising can be if you do it correctly. And I want to share with you just one of the ways that you can advertise on Facebook.

If you log in to you Facebook account and you look at the left-hand side, you'll see a tab there that says Ad Manager. You're going to want to click on that and once you do, up in the top right-hand corner, there'll be a little button that says Create a New Ad. And that's all you have to do. Once you hit that, you will be able to simply enter in the URL that you'd like to advertise and select things like what countries you want to advertise to you, what zip-codes you want to advertise to you if you're a local marketer, what states, what cities, a whole bunch of break-downs. They even break-down demographics by male or female and age groups, so you can literally track your ads - remember back to what we've just talked about at the very beginning - you can track your ads by age groups, by gender, by location and find out which advertising is working for you.

Now I'm going to suggest that when you advertise in this fashion, not only do you get to track differently, but it also decreases the costs of your advertising. Now why is that? Well think about how most people go about their advertising. They think, "I want to advertise to everybody in the United States, both male and female, all ages, and I want it to go out to this group that I'm looking at."

How many of them actually take the time to separate out their advertising by gender? By gender and age groups? What happens when you do that? What happens when you break your ad up into advertising to males in the United States age 30 to 35? Well nobody else is targeting that specific group. Your competition is not targeting that specific group, which means your ad cost goes down immediately. Because instead of competing with everybody else that's out there, you're now the most granular, you get the cheapest advertising. And, like I said at the beginning, you can track those links.

Now the great thing about Facebook ads is that it's very fast to setup all of these ad groups. You simply create one of them - so males, age 30 to 35 and you setup your URL you want it to go to and once you save that ad to create another one with all the same setting, you hit Create Similar Ad and you just go in and change the age range. That's it. And then the ad set-up. You can literally setup 18 through 90 on Facebook in all of the different ads, 10 ad groups, whatever, by just hitting Create similar Ad 9 times. So it's not a really hard or time-consuming effort in order to do that.

The other great thing about Facebook is you get to advertise based on interest. Now this is really powerful, because this is what the whole like-system on Facebook, whatever somebody puts in their profile, whatever Facebook knows about them, you get to tap into as an advertiser. So if somebody likes the Boston Red Sox and they've clicked Like on a Boston Red Sox page somewhere or if they've added that into their profile, guess what? As an advertiser, I can say I want to advertise to males in the United States, how about males in Boston Massachusetts, between the ages of 20 and 25 that already have said they like the Boston Red Sox.

Wow! All of a sudden, now think about. You already know you've got a highly targeted ad group that could literally change your business. You can do this across any type of niche on the Internet. I mean Facebook has got the most users, people like all different kinds of things and there you can do this for guitars, you can do this for remote control cars, you can do this for cooking, real estate, I don't care what your niche is, you can do this and highly, highly target your ideal customer on Facebook in just a few minutes.

We've talked about tracking your ads to get a return on your investment. This is very important and I hope that you can start doing this for your business starting today. Again, we use a tool, one of the tools we use is called link tracker and you can find out how to get that inside of the show notes.

Talked a little bit about using a 100% affiliate commission set-up or any kind of instant commission setup and we do a very specific setup that you can find out about at setupanaffiliateprogram.com. We've talked about Facebook advertising, well one way that you can use Facebook advertising.

The last thing that I want to suggest that you look into very seriously is this thing called retargeting ads. What retargeting ads do is a very powerful thing. They basically, for lack of a better word, is they stalk your best prospects anywhere they go on the Internet. Here is what I mean. If somebody comes to one of our websites, backupcreator.com for example, that visitor is automatically - let's back up a minute.

What do we know about that visitor? Well we know that they found our page either through an advertisement on the Internet, either through an affiliate on the Internet, either through word of mouth, they had heard of it, a search engine, somehow they had to take an active action in order to find themselves on our sales page, on our webpage, right?

Now what happens is once they visit our webpage, we have a service that actually tracks them, it knows who their computer is, it knows who they are and they're tapped into huge different networks of advertising.

When I say all over the Internet, I mean we've been on TV guide, we've been on the Huffington Post, Facebook, anywhere where there's Google Ads, every single ad network this is tapped into. What happens is anytime somebody that has been to our webpage now visits somewhere on the internet where there's ads that can be displayed that are part of this network, they show our ad to them.

Our ad shows up. Everywhere that they go they say "Well, there's another Backup Creator ad. There is another Backup Creator ad." Until they click on that ad, come back to our site, purchase the product. They see our product everywhere on the Internet. This does a couple of things for us. First of all, it makes us appear that we are everywhere to anybody that has been to one of our webpages.

They see our advertisements until they purchase the product. That's huge from a branding perspective and we only get charged when they actually click the link. So think about the power of that. That's huge, right? Because we're able to be in our best prospects' face until they actually buy our product.

Now when they buy, we pay for the click, it's usually about a dollar per click if that happens, they come back, hopefully they purchase and again we are able to track that so we know if we're getting a good return and they can buy.

That source that we use for that is called adroll.com, it's really simple to install, it's easy to get setup, they have got a great customer support system that will walk you through that entire process. But think for a second how powerful that would be if you use something like tracking the different ads that you are using, seeing how they're converting and then being able to show your ad to your best prospects in their face anywhere where they go on the Internet.

I hope this has changed the way that you think about the cost of advertising. And really changing how you might look at your advertising differently online. What I'm really hoping is that you start to look at not how little you're paying for advertising, but at how big of a return you're getting.

How I Escaped the Rat Race

Let's discuss why I created my own online business, why I think you should create one as well, and how hard it was for me to learn about this business because of the education that I had had, the world that I grew up in, and how being a solopreneur was so different from that.

Then we're going to set some expectation about what you can expect from me, from this podcast going forward, and also so that you can know what you're going to get out of this when you come back and listen over and over again. So we'll be right back, can't wait to share this with you and tell you about being stuck in the rat race, like you might be as well.

Having a business online is something totally different than what most of us are probably used to. I know it was for me as well. You know, one of the things that a lot of people ask me is, why did you even want to do this. Why did you want to create your own business? Actually, when I look back on it, it's a really good question.

I was sort of brought up in the IT world of corporate America. In fact, I spent ten years working at big Fortune 500 companies – companies like General Motors, Credit Suisse Financial, all of these giant companies.

Everyone around me thought that I had it made. My family thought that I was really successful, climbing the corporate ladder, my friends looked at me and thought that I had these great, stable jobs. And the truth was, well, I was dying inside. I hated having to go to work for somebody else every single day. What a lot of people saw, the stability, the paychecks, the money that I was able to make. The parts that they didn't see, well, it wasn't unusual for me to work and eighteen hour day. Wasn't unusual for me to work a twenty hour day! I wasn't able to not be tethered to a phone in my company. It wasn't unusual for me to get a phone call at two, three o'clock in the morning, after I had been at work all day, and someone would call me up and say we're having a problem with one of the systems. You need to come in and fix it.

It was great when I was younger, it was great when I was getting my life started, when I was single. In fact, I really enjoyed it to be honest, being busy, feeling important. But I found that when I got married, and got a family, and then started having kids, a lot of things changed for me.

The first thing that changed was, I had sort of moved up the corporate ladder. I was one of those cool middle manager-style people. It got to the point where a lot of the things I did, I had to justify my job and my paycheck by just sort of being around. It got to the point where the people who worked for me on my team, the systems that we were running, everything was automated. I really didn't need to be at work all of time.

I found myself just looking busy a lot. What happened was, I would go into work, usually I would try to get to work late, and when I ended up finally creating my own business and quitting my job I actually had an hour and a half commute if there was no traffic. What I would start to do is, if I left a little bit late, I would get there a little bit late. And, because my boss knew how far away I lived, nobody really thought anything of it if I showed up late.

I got really good at not getting to the office until, it started being twenty minutes late at first, then it was thirty minutes, then it was forty-five minutes late, and nobody seemed to care.

And then when I'd get to work, maybe some of you out there can relate to this, when I'd get to work I wouldn't just get in and sit down and start working right away. I had to get comfortable, I had to get coffee, I had to go talk to my friends and make sure everything was going well. You know, what they did last night, what they did that weekend.

It was really cool, because I found that if I did that, I could waste another forty-five minutes or so and nobody seemed to care.

Then I would go and sit at my desk for a while. If I had a report to do, or something to get done, I could usually get it done in fifteen minutes, thirty minutes, if I actually sat down and worked. And the rest of the time I just tried to look busy until lunch.

Then I'd go to lunch. Usually try to take a long lunch, 'cause there's always traffic, right? And then, same thing. I would come back, and the afternoon would be pretty much over, and I'd go through this every day.

It got to the point where I was just trading actual time for dollars.

I knew that if I was there while my bosses were there, while I needed to be there, I showed up. Even though I was only getting done maybe an hour or two hours at the very most of actual real work, I still had to be there for people to see my face, to think I was doing something.

It really got to me. It really started to depress me. I felt like I was wasting my life away, like I was wasting time.

When this really hit me was after my daughter was born. Once my daughter Grace was born, then I wanted to be at home, I wanted to be with my wife, I wanted to be home with my daughter. I was wasting eight hours each day, sitting in an office.

That's when I decided that I really needed to do something different. I really needed to be in charge of my own time. What I figured was, if I could work one or two hours a day for myself, but make the same income – that would be the dream, right? Actually being paid for the energy that you're putting into it? My hourly wage goes up, the amount of time that I have to spend [working] goes [down], and I could live the life that I wanted, which was watching my daughter grow up. Being able to walk her to school. Being able to do all these things.

So, being a smart IT guy, I got on this thing called Google.com and started searching for ways to have my own business at home. I started looking around the Internet, finding different websites, finding different systems, finding different programs. And what I realized was that there was a ton of ways out there to make money online.

It worked in all kinds of things. I was looking at people who were selling these things called eBooks. And I would purchase them and download them and look at them, they were basically reports, like what I was writing at work, but they were in all sorts of different topics. There were people making money selling little reports about getting in shape, losing weight, about playing guitar, about knitting. Crocheting, self-defense, everything I could think of, people were making money.

And so I thought, what do I know, what kind of skills do I have, that I can make some money at while I'm trying to learn this thing and getting it going.

I wanted to do this thing called bootstrapping. If you don't know what it is, basically, I wanted a way where I could make a little bit of money to fund my education to learn this stuff. I didn't know anything about being a solopreneur, having a business all by myself. I didn't know about all of these things that we do to sell products online.

I figured out one of the skills that I had at the time was, I knew about software. I had been in IT, I knew how to install and configure different programs, I understood how they worked, even if I didn't necessarily know that exact software system.

And I started looking around at the people that I was trying to learn stuff from. What I found out about a lot of these people that I was trying to learn stuff from was that they didn't know how to do their tech work at all. They were outsourcing it all. They were paying other people to do things!

I started looking at what they were doing, and I found one weakness that almost every single one of them had. Almost every single person that I was looking at didn't have this thing called an affiliate program. What an affiliate program is, is it basically allows people to refer sales to your website, to your online product, to your digital service.

When somebody refers a buyer, and they buy the product, they are then paid for it. It's an increased revenue for a lot of these people I was trying to learn from. And so what did I do, well, I found an affiliate program, I learned how to use it, I learned how to install it, in fact I got it down to the point where I could install it and have it all setup and configured in about thirty minutes.

And then what I would do is go to different people that I was already buying products from, and I would tell them, I've got your product, I've used it, I'm learning from it, I think it's really great. I noticed that you didn't have an affiliate program. What if I was to setup an affiliate program for you?

To my surprise, these people were very interested. Some of them I would charge, they would pay me to set it up for them. Some of them would trade me for their products and services. And so what happened was, I started to develop a relationship with these people, but I was also able to fund my education as I went along.

There are some amazing ways that you can do this now. You can do this the way that I describe for myself, there are tons of outsourcing type sites now. There's one called Fiver.com, there are other places that you can list your services that you can do for other people.

You would be amazed at the kind of things that you can get paid to do online. One of the things that comes to mind, for me, is, if you're not good at graphics – or if you are, I'm not! There are people that will pay to have graphics done, have graphics done for their blog, have graphics done for their podcast, for all these things. Approaching them, you can actually get paid to do that.

Some things that it's really easy to get paid for, if you're good at this, is writing articles for people. It's called ghost writing. Writing articles for their topic, writing blog posts for different people. Now we can leverage sort of this skill set you already have, while you're building your business.

I started to learn and get things done. One of the things I told you about, my story, at the very beginning was that I found myself with lots of extra time at work. At the job that I happened to be at, I was at a computer. So I started working on my websites while I had free time at work. That way I didn't have to spend as much time at home doing it, at night or in the morning.

Another thing that was really critical to my development and learning, and that really contributed to my success, was I told you earlier I had a commute to work. A really long commute. It was about an hour and a half each way, depending on traffic.

I listened to audio podcasts, courses that were on audio, and I would listen to them on my smartphone or I would burn them to CDs and listen to them on the way to work.

Now, think about that. I'm in the car anyway, now, instead of listening to talk radio, or listening to some music, I get to spend that three hours a day, and I don't know how long your commute is, but yours might be a little shorter, say it's an hour. But think about that. If you just listen, if your commute total was an hour a day, that's five hours a week of learning time, where you can work on your business, work on your mindset, work on your motivation, and that will move you forward.

I was learning while I was going to work, I was bootstrapping, finding ways to fund my own business and fund my education while I was working, and I was working on these sites while I had free time and while I was at work.

And a neat thing happened. I found out that the more I worked at something, the more that I learned, the easier it became. I started to develop these things called systems. If you're a solopreneur, a person working by yourself, trying to start an income stream by yourself, systems are going to be one of the most important things that you come up with. In fact, my business partner now, Robert Plank and I, everything we do, we systematize.

If we need to setup a new website, we can just grab a checklist, we don't even have to think about it, we just go through each of the steps and have it setup.

If we need to record a new podcast, same thing. We go to a system, we go through the steps, and we don't have to think or remember it.

A neat thing happens. Not only when you have a system, you'll start refining and making it better and getting faster at it, but it clears your brain out. Have you ever experienced this thing where you feel like you have information overload, you're always overwhelmed, I like to think of it as like these people run around like they're chickens with their heads cut of, they can't focus on one thing for more than two minutes because they've got all this stuff going on in their head. They're thinking about one thing, then they're thinking about something over here, and something over here, and something over here. And they never get anything done because they're always switching.

Well, if you have systems in place for everything that you do in your solopreneur business, at neat thing starts happening. Your brain becomes less cluttered. You don't have to think about things that don't matter anymore. And when you need it, you can go grab that system, put it into place, and then be done with it. You know it's right, you know it's finished, you know it's done. And you just keep refining it and refining it, and it clears out your head to learn faster. To get stuff done better. To get be able to actually enjoy your free time.

All of these things start happening. And when I started to do this, I started making a little bit of money. And the sites started working on their own, and the products started selling on their own. Because everything had been systematized to the point where traffic was coming into my websites. Products were already out there, products could be bought and delivered without me being there.

It snowballed. It started building and building and building. Until one time, I was almost to the point where I was basically making more from my online job than I was from my offline job. And I was really struggling with how to know when I should quit my day job, or if I should quit my day job.

I mean, for me, things were going along pretty good. I was basically making double my income, one from my day job, one from my online solopreneur job. But I was still just working the hours that I was at my day job.

And I couldn't figure out how to know when to quit. An interesting thing happened. Finally it came to the point where I wanted to travel. What I wanted to do was go to a seminar, an offline event where a bunch of people got together so I could learn some more about being an entrepreneur and having an offline business.

I went to my boss and said, "I need these days off. I'm going to take some vacation time, I need to go do this." My boss said to me, "You can't, we need you for a project that we're doing so I can't let you take that time off."

Something happened inside of me. Something changed. I knew at that moment that that was what I was looking for, that was the sign that I needed, if you will, to actually quit my job. And right there on the spot, I actually said, I need to resign.

My boss kind of looked at me, and I'll never forget, I mean, it was one of the best days of my life, being able to leave a six-figure job to go to a six-figure job that I had made online.

And now, I cannot tell you how amazing it is to be a solopreneur, to have a business where you can earn six figures plus day in and day out, be able to take vacations, be able to walk your daughter to school, be able to go to plays and soccer, and all of these other things that my parents weren't able to do, I can experience that with my daughter now. All because of learning how to build these businesses online.

One of these things that I want to make sure that you know about me, I do make a full-time living online. This is one hundred percent of my income, this is what I do. And the difference is that what I want to do over the next coming weeks and months of this podcast, I want to share with you some of these systems that I use, and some of the mindset. Some of the ways that you can be more productive.

I firmly believe that every one of you can have the lifestyle that you want, the business that you want, the free time that you want, and really that happiness that you want and deserve. But the thing that is missing is that you need to be retrained.

Corporate America does a weird thing to us, just like it did to me. It teaches you that you get paid for not being productive. What I want to teach you is how to think like an entrepreneur, how to develop systems, some that I'm going to share with you, so that you can become more productive and move forward with your business to achieve the dreams that you have.

That's really what this book is about. It's about starting your own business, about building your own business, if you've already got one, and about becoming more productive so that you really can live that dream of being able to have the lifestyle that you want.

Three Secrets to Explode the Growth of Your Business

I was reading some emails from my list and I realized that there is an important lesson that few people talk about when trying to build an online business. It was something that was very powerful for me personally.

When a lot people are getting started with their home-based, small business they want to do everything themselves. The want to be completely self-reliant.

That's a terrible goal to have for a couple of reasons.

Building a Business Is LONELY. Having a person to reach out to and share your successes and failures with is vital.

If you don't have friends that understand what you are doing your going to end up sitting at your desk for 20 hours a day and you're going to be miserable.

Even worse, you are going to sacrifice your relationships with your friends and family. You need someone that understands your excitement when you make progress.

If you don't build relationships with people that understand what you are building, you are just setting yourself up for failure.

Don't Try To Do Everything Yourself. A lot of people miss the boat here. They want to learn and do it all themselves. I am not saying that you shouldn't keep learning.

For me personally, I learn better through doing. So I need to find people that I can emulate. The key to fast growth in your business is to find people with different skill sets than you that you can learn from.

Accountability. It doesn't matter if you actually have a real "partner." Just make a list of 4 things that you can accomplish today and write it down.

Why Some People Make It and Others Don't

Things change in internet marketing very quickly.

Things like the FTC cracking down, things like MasterCard and Visa completely changing their rules, shutting off major marketers' accounts, and I think that this is actually a very good thing. And what's sad to me is that I've been getting emails from people, telling me that they're broke, telling me that they don't know how they're going to purchase any products, telling me that they need training but that they don't have any money, whatsoever. And frankly, this confuses me because you're all building businesses on the internet.

And so, I wanted to talk to you guys a little bit today about why you're probably feeling that you're broke, why you're feeling that you're not there, and what I really blame for all of this is the general mistrust in the marketplace. I don't blame you, guys. I mean I don't think the problem is that you're broke. You all are sending messages from your Blackberry's, you're all on the internet, you have internet connections, you have computers, you're actually trying to build something, but I think that you're going about it in the wrong way, and I don't think that it's your fault.

It's Not Your Fault

What's the point in me telling you all this? Well, what I really want to get across to you guys is that this feeling that you have, this doubt that you guys are having. This skepticism towards internet marketing and making money on the internet is not your fault.

How did you even get started with an online business? I mean I don't think that typically most people are sitting around at home, they think one day, "Oh, you know what would be really great is to make a few extra bucks online." And so, what do you do? Well, if you're probably like me, you did some sort of like quick search on the internet and found your way eventually to some sort of squeeze page, and we're all familiar with this by this point – those cool little pages where you go and they offer you some free gift in exchange for your email address and name.

So typically, what happens is you got home, do a quick little search on the internet, end up on one of these squeeze pages with this great sounding offer, you put in your name and email address, and the next thing you know is that you've got a bunch of people telling you every single day in your inbox that they're making all of this money online and that it's so completely easy, and they basically bombard you, but what happens is you get so many of these messages over and over and over again where you really started out with a very realistic thought process. You started out thinking, "if I could make a few extra bucks, I could actually build something up, wouldn't it be cool if I had an extra $100, $200?"

This Could Work!

But you got caught in this whole sales funnel and the next thing you know, you went from thinking you could make an extra 100 or 200 bucks to you could make all of this cash, retire rich, sit on the beach in your underwear, and mix drinks all day. Unfortunately, you start to think that this could work. You actually at some point start to believe that you could literally wake up the next morning and have millions of dollars in your bank account, and I hate to be the one to break this to you, but it's not going to happen that way.

In fact, if you think that way right now, I'm going to give you the best tip you've ever got. Stop, change your email address, don't read any more marketing, and go save your money and spend it on something good. Spend time with your family, spend time doing things that actually matter to you because it's never going to happen. I mean if that happened, if it was that easy, then everybody would be rich on the internet and nobody would be saying that they're broke or having all these doubts.

So, if you're buying that dream, I'm here to tell you right now, it may not be what you want to hear, but it's the truth.

And then what starts happening is the next thing you know, daily, you start getting the same emails from all of these major people, or who appear to be major, telling you about this great product. That their friend just released something really really cool, and because you don't know any better, you believe them. You go and buy the product, and it leads you to some professionally written sales page where you spend all day reading these sales letters, believing this hype.

I mean these are professionally written 20, 30-page letters that are designed to draw you in, that are designed to sell you on that sort of dream. And what ends up happening is you end up jumping from product to product to product because every week, there's a new launch and every week, you get all of these emails telling you that this is the next thing, this is the next thing, this is the next thing.

Have You Noticed A Pattern?

This never stops. It's an endless cycle. And it's all of the people getting together, sending you out these launch emails and when you see those emails, the first time you made your scheme over it. But then when you open up the next email and it's got a different subject line but it's the same message or for the same product, you start to think about it. And then by the third, fourth, fifth, sixth time that you see the exact same offer from a different person, you automatically think in your head, "Well all of these people are saying that this is so great, it must be." And then you go and buy it, and typically you're disappointed, you do nothing with it, and then you move on to the next big product, and they catch you in the cycle. And unfortunately, that's the truth about what is happening to you.

So, I don't believe that you're broke. I believe that you're not believing in people, that you don't believe any of the hype anymore, and as you well shouldn't. So, the other problem is you're spending all of this time, you're spending all of this money, and you're only actually using a small fraction, if any, of the stuff that you bought. I know when I got started, I spent thousands of dollars with all of these major gurus, with all of these promises, and luckily, I ran into some pretty good guys early on who stirred me in a better direction and showed me that there were actually some good people online, some honest people online, and sort of let me know what was happening and why I was seeing all of these offers that I was seeing.

You Want A Magic Button?

The other thing is that they've sold you on looking for a "magic button." Again, like I said, I mean if you honestly believe that you're going to wake up tomorrow with millions of dollars in your bank account, stop doing internet marketing right now. You're not building a business. There's no business offline that generates that kind of cash. Why would you think it would be any different online?

The truth is – is that it's not. We are in a unique situation, we do have global reach, and we can build businesses from our house. But you need to be realistic. Remember, where you started from, it was probably with just making a couple extra bucks. And now suddenly, you've got this fascination that you've got to make millions of dollars and be rich. Well, it's just simply not going to happen. So, the worst part about all of these cheap emails that you're getting, these products that you're buying is that you don't even know these people. You don't know anything about them. Most of them never even show their face. They don't have any products. Some of them don't even have blogs. So, I mean why would you feel compelled to spend money with this type of people? Maybe you should think about that real carefully.

Think About This

I want to give you something to think about here. What would it take to educate yourself to start a business offline? I mean do you honestly believe that if you are going to go offline and start a business, you could just sign a paper, turn it on, and it would start happening? It's not that case. I mean I think that we'll agree.

Think about how much higher education costs. I know at least in America, it can run up to $30,000 a year or more. It's not a cheap proposition, and people do that just to go work for the 9 to 5 grind.

Think about how much time, effort, and money it would take to actually start a successful offline business. It's not something that you could do with no cash flow. It's not something that you could just start up on a credit card. It's something that you would have to seriously sit down, think about, plan for, and start it.

And the thing is – is that it's no different online.

I hate to be the one to break that to you but there's no difference online except that there's fewer overhead and fewer tools that you need, and you can actually, with a single person or two people, start a very very successful business, but there still are expenses that you're going to have to take. And unfortunately, a lot of it is going to be in education. I personally pay thousands of dollars a year to meet with my mentor three times a year to talk to him for 45 minutes – 45 minutes three times a year. I travel all over the country just to get those 45 minutes and some people think I'm crazy for doing that but I say that the investment is paid for itself over and over and over again.

3 Types Of Marketers

So, what I want to tell you guys, the point of all this is that from my experience, the short time that I've been online, I've noticed that there's basically three types of marketers, and just knowing this is going to put you ahead of the game.

The Dream Seller

So, the first type of marketer and unfortunately probably the type that you most early ran into when you were getting started online with your business is the ones that "sell the dream," and these are the people that basically do what I was telling you about earlier, where they coordinate the giant launches, they coordinate together where they're all sending massive amounts of emails for the same product on the same day over and over and over again. And quite frankly, they just do this in a rotation. And if you actually start watching and seeing it, I think that you'll pick up on it. So, they are basically selling the dream and the truth is – is a lot of the claims they make, they could probably achieve those results, but the problem is you don't have the connections, you don't have the sized list, and you really need to think about keeping it realistic.

Fake It Till You Make It

The second type of marketer that I've ran into online and unfortunately, I almost think that this marketer is more dangerous than the "selling the dream" marketer, and this is the "fake it till you make a crowd." These are the people that always are talking about numbering, always talking about statistics, but never ever showing any sort of proof for it. I'm sure that you have run across these types before.

They're very good at talking a big game, but when it really comes down to it, have they ever shown you any real proof? The other problem with the "fake it till you make a crowd" and one way that I always can spot these people is that they never talk about their failures. They never talk about their failures. I mean it would be impossible to think that somebody never has a failure online, that they never have a product that launches that didn't go well.

Unfortunately, a lot of these people are at sort of the mid-level, I'll say, in marketing where you don't know what they make. They make these outrageous income claims, it goes up and up and up, and unfortunately, like I actually know some of these people, and I know that their list aren't as big as they claim they are, I know that for a fact that their income isn't as big as they say it is. And so, I would really encourage you to take a close look at the people that are telling you about what great product creators they are, how much they know about memberships sites. If you look around and they have no membership sites, if they have no products – I mean this red flag should be going off everywhere.

I mean the other day I saw an email come across from somebody who was claiming to be a master product creator, and then I went and looked and they didn't have a single product. So, how do they have such a great product creation system and how are they such a good product creator if they have no products? It's totally baffling. So, you don't even really have to dig deep to find these people, but just do a little bit of due diligence and figure out if these people are telling you the truth or not.

The Honest Entrepreneur

Luckily, there is a third type of marketer that I've run across, and these are the honest entrepreneurs. These are the people that are actually "walking the walk." These are the people that are actually doing what they say and providing real value to their customers. Because let's face it, the truth is is that there are people out there that are making good incomes online from doing the right thing. And the real trick is just to find those people and hunt them out. Unfortunately, for most people, they never actually get to find those people because the hype sells much better.

The Light At The End Of The Tunnel

Luckily for you, at least there is a light at the end of the tunnel. The first thing is that just realizing how this game works and not there's three types of marketers out there. It's going to put you in an infinitely better position to plan out your business, to understand the types of people that you want to be taking advice from, and to actually figure out which type of person you want to be, and I hope that every one of you is choosing to go on the path of the honest entrepreneur.

Look at the marketing you're receiving, look at the emails that you're getting, look at the way that they're marketing to you, and figure out if you're getting any value from it. I mean I know a lot of people that are just on all of these lists, like they get thousands of emails every single day and it's just from people going, "here's my free thing, here's my free thing, here's my free thing," and then typically, they'll buy something eventually.

If these people don't even have their own products, if they aren't teaching you anything, they're just sending you links to go sign up to somebody else's list, I mean what value is there in that? I mean you can study all day, but the fact is until you take action online, you're not going to make any money and you're not going to improve your situation. Figure out if you trust these people. I mean I'm not saying like go do a massive research on them, but see if they have a blog, see if you can see anything about them, see the crowd that they run with, see if you can figure out if these people are actually worth you even reading their emails. And if they're not, just get rid of them.

There are honest people making real money on the internet. It's your job to seek those people out. I've given you some of the information that I have learned in my short time online and how to identify these people, understanding that they're out there, and I'm hoping that since you're on my list, reading my blog, you're not going to get caught in the sort of traps that I see people getting caught in out there.

The Easiest, Fastest, and Most Proven Way to Setup Your Online Business in 3 Days or Less...

"Go from Internet Marketing Beginner to Expert In This 3-Day Online Bootcamp"

By the end of this 3-day training, you'll have the following setup:

- Niche & Domain
- Blog & Social Proof
- Web Page
- Sales Letter

- Email Optin Page
- Membership Site
- Autoresponder
- Traffic

You Followed Along And Created Everything You Need: A Complete Online Business!

You've always dreamed of telling your friends about your web site. Dreamed of firing your boss and quitting your day job. Dreamed of working less, making more, and retiring early.

The technical stuff is out of the way. You can now focus on your marketing and your passion.

Let's get you setup and making money!

Discover more here: http://www.IncomeMachine.com

10483420R00088

Made in the USA
San Bernardino, CA
15 April 2014